STUDENT VOICE IN SCHOOL REFORM

STUDENT VOICE IN SCHOOL REFORM

Building Youth-Adult Partnerships
That Strengthen Schools and Empower Youth

— ◆ —

Dana L. Mitra

STATE UNIVERSITY OF NEW YORK PRESS

KH

Cover image: Chris Schmidt/istockphoto

Published by
State University of New York Press, Albany

For information, contact State University of New York Press, Albany, NY
www.sunypress.edu

Production by Judith Block and Marilyn Semerad
Marketing by Michael Campochiaro

Library of Congress Cataloging in Publication Data

Mitra, Dana L.
  Student voice in school reform : Building youth-adult partnerships
that strengthen schools and empower youth / Dana L. Mitra.
      p. cm.
  Includes bibliographical references and index.
  ISBN 978-0-7914-7319-1 (hardcover : alk. paper)
  ISBN 978-0-7914-7320-7 (pbk. : alk. paper)
  1. High school students—United States. 2. Student participation in
administration—United States. 3. Educational change—United States.
I. Title.

LA229.M58 2007
373.18—dc22

                                                            2007013149

10 9 8 7 6 5 4 3 2 1

8/28/09

*For the youth at Whitman High School
and Kaden and Carson, whose births
inspired the creation of this book*

CONTENTS

ACKNOWLEDGMENTS

This work would not have been possible without the cooperation and support of students and staff at Whitman High School. I was inspired by the vision and commitment of Sean and Amy. Whitman students, including Lata, Rosalinda, and Joey, reminded me constantly of why I returned to graduate school and why I wanted to write this book. They possessed wisdom beyond their years and spirits that could not be dampened.

Milbrey McLaughlin provided intellectual support to explore these ideas. Her belief in the value of this research and encouragement throughout the way pushed my thinking beyond writer's block to keep me focused on the true meaning in my data. I am grateful for her generosity, her counsel, and her friendship. Jim Greeno provided many hours of counsel on theory and on sharing experiences from Whitman. Ray McDermott posed intellectual challenges and tough questions to push me to question my assumptions and stand my ground when necessary. Mike Copland offered encouragement and a willingness to travel to be a part of this endeavor. I also gained significant insight through multiple conversations with Joan Talbert and the rest of my colleagues at the Center for Research on the Context of Teaching. They provided feedback on my work, taught me about other schools in the region, and offered ongoing information and encouragement. Thank you especially to Becky Crowe Hill for introducing me to the work at Whitman and to Wendy Lin, who provided survey support.

My friends along the way helped me not only to think about education and schooling but also about how to combine the life of a researcher with the many other aspects of life that make this work worthwhile. My data group—Ginger Cook, Sarah Deschenes, Matt Kelemen, and Misty Sato—pushed me to move beyond the fear of tackling my huge pile of raw data and moved me beyond complacency to question my assumptions. Amy Hightower, Ben Justice, Sam Bersola, and Angela Schmiede painstakingly read my drafts and taught me much about research, grammar, and keeping a sense of humor. Kim Powell and Laura Post provided intellectual and emotional support, including advice on working with faculty members, thinking about theory, and keeping things in perspective. Rebecca Carver was my intellectual fellow traveler and was instrumental in guiding me toward a framework for explaining the youth development outcomes. Her light and vision in this world will be greatly missed.

Ann Lieberman encouraged me to pursue publication of this text and helped me to think of how to go about doing so. Lisa Chesnel championed my cause at State University of New York Press and encouraged me to persist with pursuing publication for this manuscript.

The Hewlett and Stuart Foundations provided financial support to conduct this research. Penn State University's College of Education provided financial support to write the final manuscript.

My greatest gratitude goes to my parents, who inspired me by their example and who have been my staunchest supporters always. To Kaden, who provided me with a reason to make the final push to finish the initial draft of this book and to Carson, who provided me the time to focus on polishing the work. Both remind me constantly of the true meaning and spirit of life. And most important, to Todd, who offered unwavering support, confidence, understanding, and love every step of the way.

Chapter 1

INTRODUCTION

Many youth in today's high schools share the desperation of Rosalinda Gutierrez, a tenth grade student at Whitman High School, who exclaimed, "They don't even see how students feel at this school. We're really dying inside." In fact, students report that adults rarely listen to their views, and they rarely involve students in important decisions. Large numbers of high school students describe their school experiences in terms of anonymity and powerlessness (Noddings, 1992; Poplin & Weeres, 1992; Heath & McLaughlin, 1993; Nightingale & Wolverton, 1993). Large school size, the segregation by age and ability, and a view of students as "clients" further increase the sense of distance between teachers and students. To make matters worse, these experiences of alienation often result in disengagement between students and their schools. In fact, disengagement is a key reason for students dropping out of school, according to a 2006 survey (Bridgeland, Dilulio, & Morison, 2006). Disengaged students tend to come to school less, have lower self-concepts, and achieve less academically and are more likely to drop out of school (Fullan, 2001; Rudduck & Wallace, 1997).

Ironically, youth themselves tend to be viewed as the source of the problem. Teenagers are portrayed by the media, politicians, and even researchers as uniformly resistant, rebellious, and determined to isolate themselves from society (Males, 1996; Takanishi, 1993). The consequence of this perception is that it limits the expectations not only of adults but also of adolescents.

What might happen if we viewed youth as part of the solution, rather than as part of the problem? This book examines the emergence of "student voice" as an avenue for fostering both youth development and broader conceptions of school leadership aimed at achieving meaningful school change. More than a token gesture of a student sitting in on a meeting, student voice activities are school-based youth-adult partnerships (Camino, 2000; Jones & Perkins, 2004). When placed into practice, student voice can describe instances in which young people collaborate with adults to address the problems in their schools and to improve teaching and learning in their classrooms.

Previous research has identified important benefits of student voice initiatives for schools, youth, and adults. Such efforts can serve as a catalyst for change in schools, including helping to improve teaching, curriculum, and teacher-student relationships and leading to changes in student assessment and teacher training (Fielding, 2001; Rudduck & Flutter, 2000). Student voice initiatives also have been shown to increase youth agency, to create greater attachment to schools, and to build a range of skills and competencies, including learning to get along with others, planning complex projects, and public speaking (Kirshner, O'Donoghue, & McLaughlin, 2003; Mitra, 2004). In addition to the professional growth that these partnerships can facilitate, these student voice initiatives also benefit the adults involved by fulfilling a fundamental psychosocial need of adult development by fostering intergenerational relationships that include sharing knowledge and experiences with youth (Ginwright, 2005).

Much of the previous research on topics related to student voice has looked at classroom-level student voice initiatives, including the importance of joint student-teacher responsibility for creating the learning environment (McLaughlin, Talbert, Kahne, & Powell, 1990; Meyer, 1999) and the examination of the power relationship between students and teachers (Blase, 1991; Cusick, 1973; Muncey & McQuillan, 1991; Powell, Farrar, & Cohen, 1985). In contrast, few examples exist of student voice as a new conception of school leadership and an avenue toward influencing schoolwide change.

With little research available on the resurgence of student voice efforts occurring for the first time since the early seventies, the intent in this study was to find a "best case" scenario of student voice efforts. This research provided an in-depth explanation of a school that did contain strong student voice efforts. While many high schools have struggled with how to improve student outcomes, Whitman decided to go straight to the source and ask the students. The students accepted the task with gusto and sought, in their terms, to make the partnership "real"—meaning that students wanted their school to hear their voices. They wanted to engage in meaningful discussions about why so many students at Whitman failed their classes and dropped out of school. They wanted to partner with their teachers and principals to improve learning for themselves and their peers.

The research sample for this book is based on representativeness of the concept of 'student voice' (Strauss & Corbin, 1990), rather than representativeness of school sites. The goal was to maximize the opportunities to observe student involvement by choosing the sites that most actively demonstrated commitment to working with students on their reform work rather than to find schools with a range of student involvement in reform efforts. This book therefore tells the story of "Whitman High School" (all names have been changed in this book), a school serving families who rarely have a voice in schools in the United States. Located in a bedroom community in northern California, Whitman High School serves a community comprised of first-generation immigrants from Latin America and Asia as well as working-class African Americans and European Americans. Half of Whitman High School's students are English-language learners, and half qualify for the free or reduced-price lunch program.

With the school graduating just over half (57%) of the students that start in ninth grade, and with one-third of its teachers electing to leave each year, Whitman High School staff felt compelled to make changes. In 1998, Whitman received a major grant to launch a three-year reform effort from the Bay Area School Reform Collaborative (BASRC), a $112 million education initiative in the San Francisco Bay area that was supported by the Annenberg Challenge and the Hewlett Foundation. As a part of deciding where to focus their reform efforts, the school's reform leadership team made the unusual decision of asking students what they felt needed to be improved.

During the time that this research was conducted, Whitman could easily be considered the trailblazer on student involvement in the San Francisco Bay Area. Many other high schools in the area were talking about wanting to involve students in their reform work, particularly through interviewing focus groups of students. After conducting a small sample of interviews and observations with other schools and after talking with school reform consultants in the area, it was clear, however, that although these other schools indicated an interest in increasing student voice, it was not occurring at these schools at the time. The student voice effort happening at Whitman was unusual and deserved to be the sole focus of this study.

This book focuses on the work of Whitman's student voice initiative, Student Forum. The group began when a fourth-year English teacher selected a cross-section of students to participate in focus groups on how improve the academic success of ninth graders. This group of 30 students continued to work together after the focus groups to target its efforts at increasing student participation in efforts to reform the school and to institute new school programs and policies. Student Forum sought to inject student voice into school decision making and to seek ways to make the school a better place for all students. The group eventually narrowed its focus to one schoolwide issue—building communication and partnership between students and teachers.

This book describes the evolution of student voice at Whitman High School. Specifically, the book examines two questions: What does student voice look like in practice? and What difference does it make? The first half of the book focuses on the nitty gritty of how student voice evolved at Whitman High School. It contributes needed research on what student voice initiatives look like in practice, including supports that enable them and detractors that constrain them. Chapter 2 provides a background on previous student voice research. Chapter 3 describes Whitman students and the school's reform history that culminated in the initial step of fostering student voice at Whitman—adults listening to students through interviews and surveys. Chapter 4 examines the process by which Student Forum members wanted to make a difference in their school and tried to figure out how to do so. The youth translated their vision of student voice into a structure and a plan that would allow them to foster a youth-adult partnership at the school. Chapter 5 lays out how hard work of creating Student Forum finally led to action as the group implemented many activities intended to increase communication and build partnership between students and teachers. The chapter describes the leadership assumed by Whitman youth as they sought to make changes in their schools and communities. Their actions demonstrated a rare occasion in which young people assumed much of the responsibility for making changes happen.

The second half of the book considers the difference that student voice made at Whitman and the connections between this research and educational leadership, professional learning communities, and positive youth development. Chapter 6 examines how student voice initiatives can expand notions of distributed leadership, professional learning communities, and collaboration to include young people in conversations and efforts to achieve educational change. Student Forum demonstrates the potential for strengthening school improvement by broadening a school's learning community to include students in the reform process.

Chapter 7 defines the fundamental ways in which student voice initiatives can lead to important gains in positive youth development outcomes for youth. In a time in which students feel increasingly isolated and disengaged from school, the chapter provides powerful evidence of ways in which young people can increase their sense of agency, a range of skills necessary for leading successful lives, and the growth of relationships that increase their attachment. Chapter 8 concludes the book by reiterating the important lessons that Whitman offers scholars, policy makers, and practitioners.

Chapter 2

UNDERSTANDING THE HISTORY AND OUTCOMES OF STUDENT VOICE INITIATIVES

In recent years, educational researchers have begun examining how an increase in student voice in schools can improve the ways in which youth can have the opportunity to participate in school decisions that will shape their lives and the lives of their peers (Fielding, 2001; Goodwillie, 1993; Levin, 2000). Otherwise referred to as "student participation," "active citizenship," "youth leadership," "youth empowerment" and "pupil voice," student voice is the ways in which young people can work with teachers and administrators to cocreate the path of reform. This process can enable youth to meet their own developmental needs and can strengthen student ownership of the educational reform process.

When placed into practice, student voice can range from the most basic level of youth sharing their opinions of problems and potential solutions to allowing young people to collaborate with adults to address the problems in their schools to youth taking the lead on seeking change (Mitra, 2005). All types of student voice, from limited input to substantial leadership, are considerably different from the types of roles that students typically perform in U.S. schools (such as planning school dances and holding pep rallies). Stronger forms of student voice initiatives can be considered "youth-adult partnerships" (Camino, 2000), which are defined as relationships in which both youth and adults have the potential to contribute to decision-making processes, to learn from one another, and to promote change (Jones & Perkins, 2004). Youth-adult partnerships employ the elements of power sharing among youth and adults, giving each party a valued voice and vote in terms of decision making. Collaboration comes with an expectation of youth sharing the responsibility for the vision of the group, the activities planned, and the group process that facilitates the enactment of these activities (Jones, 2004). This process forges youth-adult partnerships as collaborative learning environments where individuals come together in groups, with the willingness to share authority, accept responsibility, and highlight individual members' abilities and contributions (Panitz, 1996). A focus on mutual teaching and learning develops in youth-adult partnerships as all parties involved assume a leadership role in some aspects of their shared effort. The transfer of skills between adults and youth takes place through appropriate guidance and coaching by adults (Camino, 2000).

STUDENT VOICE PAST AND PRESENT

The subject of student voice in school reform and decision making traces back to the creation of student government in 1894 at George Junior Republic School in Freeville, New York (Johnson, 1991). Student government was created to provide students with an opportunity to practice the duties and responsibilities of citizenship in a democracy, but school administrators rarely afforded students the opportunity to grapple with core issues in the school process. Instead, student governments most often have focused on periph-eral issues such as social activities and student volunteering efforts.

    This attitude changed in the late 1960s when a new concep-tion of student power arose as a result of other social movements. During this era, student governments in some schools positioned themselves in an adversarial relationship to school administration. Such a focus continued in the 1970s as students around the coun-try sought to liberate themselves from what they perceived to be "oppressive authority." During this time, the National Education Association (NEA) suggested that genuine student voice is indeed "possible if students are guaranteed certain basic rights, including right to free inquiry and expression, right to due process, right to freedom of association, right to freedom of peaceful assembly and petition, right to participate in their governance of the school, col-lege and university, right to freedom from discrimination, and right to educational opportunity" (Johnson, 1991, p. 7). Similar pronouncements were made at conferences around the country (such as Ferguson, 1970) as this conception of student empower-ment took hold. During this time, changes did happen as students in many communities won seats on local school boards.

The tide turned in the late 1970s and, since then, in most schools student voice has dwindled to little but the ceremonial election of student council officers. Student governments, as they have existed for the past one hundred years, have rarely concerned themselves with meaningful issues in schools (Johnson, 1991; Schmuck & Schmuck, 1990). Most student governments exercise little power, focus primarily on social activities, and do not represent a cross-section of the school. In fact, a nationwide study of communities found no instances where student governments engaged in formal problem solving related to either the "school's academic program or social-emotional climate. In most places, administrators told us that student council was ineffective, if not inoperative" (Schmuck & Schmuck, 1990, p. 19).

From *The Nation at Risk* manifesto in the late 1980s to today, the topic of student voice still gets little if any mention in national school reform agendas. Although the 1990s did see an increase in discussions of communitywide solutions to school problems, the discussions rarely extended to the role of students. As the current focus on closing the achievement gap and improving student achievement grows, the voices of individual actors have become more subdued. Perhaps then it is no surprise that Michael Fullan's 2001 review of the student role in reform found that little has changed in the past twenty years.

BROADENING COLLABORATION AND DISTRIBUTING LEADERSHIP

Despite the current political emphases in education, student voice initiatives have been slowly growing in pockets across the United States and in Australia, the United Kingdom, and Canada. These efforts have not been geared to rights and empowerment as in the past. Instead, they focus on the benefits of student participation for schools by suggesting that school reform will be more successful if students participate. This new form of student voice broadens the educational conceptions of professional collaboration and distributed leadership to include students as members of school-based learning communities.

Research on these new initiatives demonstrates how schools benefit from including students in the reform process by including them in the professional learning communities that engage school personnel in exchanging ideas, providing support, offering critiques, and sharing expertise (Leonard & Leonard, 2001; McLaughlin & Talbert, 2001). Professional collaboration has long been shown to lead to improved teaching and learning as teachers work together to critique practice, to support professional growth, and to learn together how to improve practice (Grossman, Wineburg, & Woolworth, 2001; Lieberman & Grolnick, 2001; Louis & Kruse, 1995; Newmann, King, & Youngs, 2001; McLaughlin & Talbert, 2001; Talbert, 1995). Student voice in such collaborations have led to some incredible accomplishments, including improvements in instruction, curriculum, and teacher-student relationships (Soohoo, 1993); changes in school policy, such as abolishing unfair testing policies (Colatos & Morrell, 2003); changes in teacher preparation (Cook-Sather, 2001); and changes assessment systems (Fielding, 2001).

Student voice initiatives also have much to contribute to the growing body of literature emphasizing the value of extending the notion of distributed leadership (Elmore, 2000; Lashway, 2003) to include students in the decision-making process. Research has demonstrated that youth-adult partnerships can create a synergy that transcends what youth or adults alone can do, including sparking great strides in an organization's vision and accomplishments (Kirshner, O'Donoghue, & McLaughlin, 2002; Mitra, 2001; National Research Council, 2002; Zeldin, 2004; Zeldin, Camino, & Mook, 2005). Increasing student voice in schools also can encourage schools to more closely align their mission, goals, and activities with a social justice focus. Research indicates that young people tend to broach subjects that adults are reluctant to discuss, such as equity issues that tend to get swept under the rug by administrators and other adults in the school who would rather avoid controversy (Fine, 1991; Wehlage, Rutter, Smith, Lesko, & Fernandez, 1989). For example, by involving students in schoolwide discussions about academic achievement—and particularly students failing subjects or rarely attending school—school personnel cannot easily shift the blame of failure onto the students (Mitra, 2003). Instead they must assess the problems within the school's structure and culture. Giving students a voice in such reform conversations reminds teachers and administrators that students possess unique knowledge and perspectives about their schools that adults cannot fully replicate without this partnership (Kushman, 1997; Levin, 2000; Mitra,

2007; Rudduck & Wallace, 1997; Thorkildsen, 1994). Furthermore, school personnel are learning that youth have access to information and relationships that teachers and administrators do not, such as providing a bridge between the school and families reluctant to interact with school personnel, including first generation immigrant families (Mitra, 2006).

OPPORTUNITIES FOR YOUTH DEVELOPMENT

Youth-adult partnerships such as student voice initiatives have been shown to have powerful benefits for the young people involved. Research has found young people who participate in youth-adult partnerships tend to have an increase in confidence and leadership and attachment to social institutions and to foster a range of competencies (Kirshner, O'Donoghue, & McLaughlin, 2002; Larson, Walker, & Pearce, 2005; Zeldin, Camino, & Calvert, 2002). Research conducted with middle-school students in the United States also found that students valued their schooling the most when their teachers heard their voices and "honored" them (Oldfather, 1995).

Increasing student voice in schools additionally has been shown to help to reengage alienated students by providing them with a stronger sense of ownership in their schools. Psychological research has demonstrated the connection between autonomy and motivation. If an individual has a sense of control over her environment, she will feel more intrinsically motivated to participate (Johnson, 1991). By providing new opportunities to increase collaborative interactions between students and adults and to engage students in actively shaping their own learning environments, increasing student voice can help to reengage alienated students by creating a sense of ownership in the school and building a source of intrinsic motivation (deCharms, 2001).

Student voice initiatives also can provide a rare opportunity to point out value in a diverse range of talents and leadership styles (Camino & Zeldin, 2000; Denner, Meyer, & Bean 2005), including being a critical thinker, teacher, anchor, peacemaker, and supporter. Each person has something to learn from the others (Camino, 2000). Students can learn a broad range of competencies, including physical, intellectual, psychological, emotional, and social skills, and opportunities to develop social and cultural capital (Camino, 2000; Camino & Zeldin, 2000; Larson, Miller, & Pearce, 2005; Perkins & Borden, 2003; Zeldin, Camino, Calvert, & Ivey, 2002).

OVERCOMING BARRIERS TO DEVELOPING STUDENT VOICE INITIATIVES

Despite the potential benefits of student voice initiatives, the institutional constraints of schools prove to be especially challenging to puncture because the power and status distinctions in school settings especially provide a dramatic form of asymmetry—especially due to commonly held norms of deference to adult authority and the separation of adults and youth roles in schools. The institutionalized roles of teachers and students in school contradict much of what an adult-youth partnership is about, and within the walls of schools, adult and youth very often fall back to their expected teacher/student roles, even when they are intentionally trying to foster new types of relationships. Perhaps it is not surprising then that student voice initiatives are uncommon. Creating a new set of working conditions that could foster youth-adult partnerships requires creating new norms, developing developing new relationships, and new organizational structures within them (Della Porta & Diani, 1995; Oakes & Lipton, 2002). Youth-adult partnerships must develop new scripts to learn how to work together in equitable ways, as well as to convince others of their views and thus garner support for their efforts and to counter oppositional frames that run contrary to their efforts (Binder, 2002; Gamson, 1992; Snow & Benford, 1992).

To combat these challenges, successful student voice initiatives must involve a process by which youth become empowered and adults learn to share the power that they hold. True engagement requires a "rupture of the ordinary" (Fielding, 2004), which demands as much of teachers as it does of students. Benjamin Kirshner (2003) has examined similar questions in efforts to build youth-adult partnerships in community-based organizations. He found that students and adults struggled with power relationships and how best to delegate responsibilities to students. The collective also wrestled with how to provide opportunities for all members to participate. A further struggle occurred in deciding whose ideas should be presented when there was a disagreement between students and adults.

Roger Holdsworth and Pat Thomson (2002) suggest that teachers and others concerned about student participation need to think critically about the spaces in which democratic projects and programs can occur. Some strategies for increasing student participation are better conducted within the formal structures of schools, and others are better conducted outside of the formal system through community-based organizations and other such formats. For example, the youth participation newsletter in Australia, *Connect*, survives only by subscription and unpaid labor. Holdsworth and Thomson believe that *Connect* would not be possible if it was formally supported by a school or the government because of its often critical stance of public policy. They conclude that student voice can support democratic activity, but more often than not, it is a thin, conservative democracy in which advantage students assume all of the rights to voice. In such cases, student voice is a façade of participation and consultation. Thus attention must be paid not only to having student voice heard, but also to paying attention to which voices are being heard when given the opportunity.

One issue that youth-adult partnerships must watch vigilantly is whether they increase the voices of the disadvantaged or if they only raise the voice of privileged youth. Elena Silva's research (2003) provides an example of student voice gone bad. She describes the story of a school that asked students to be a part of the planning team that was preparing for a whole-school review for certification purposes. While students were invited to the table, their suggestions were ignored and participating students felt disrespected and silenced. The failed effort demonstrated that student voice entails more than appointing students on a committee. Such gestures result in merely tokenism if student opinions are not valued and incorporated as a part of the power structure of the reform. In Silva's research, students of color began to drop out of student panel working to provide the school with recommendations for their accreditation process. In the end, the group was comprised primarily of wealthier white females. The students of color that were still present in the group tended to defer to these vocal, privileged women in the group. While not a focus of the research, Silva's piece also supports Patricia Bauch and Ellen Goldring's (1998) assertion that adults need to be empowered in order to allow an increase in the empowerment of others. The teachers and administrators in this reform effort demonstrated an inability to focus on the details of the reform work themselves because they had insufficient time, resources, and supportive relations to engage in the task. Thus, they were unable to complete their tasks sincerely, let alone involve students as well.

LOOKING AHEAD

Because of the difficulty of establishing student voice initiatives, an understanding of the conditions that enable and constrain them is needed. Any educational change is hard, but changing the roles of students is extremely hard because it pushes against strongly held institutional beliefs about the roles of young people in schools. Even when a school is committed to collaboration in principle, an inclusion of stakeholder voices is nevertheless difficult to achieve in practice (cf. Epstein & Sanders, 1999; Swap, 1993).

This book takes up this charge by taking a deep look at how Whitman High School went about the process of partnering with students in their reform process. The remaining chapters in the first half of this book detail how Student Forum evolved into a youth-adult partnership at Whitman High School. Despite the inevitable struggles for legitimacy, the teachers and students learned to work together to try to improve communication at a very troubled school. Along the way, the group achieved marked gains in pushing the school toward being a more positive and welcoming place for students and teachers. Additionally, the young people and adults involved in the student voice efforts experienced enormous personal growth.

Chapter 3

LISTENING TO STUDENTS

It's graduation day for Whitman High School's class of 2000. I race into the classrooms where the soon-to-be graduates are lining up for the ceremony. After two years of field research at the school, I have come to know and hold in high regard many members of the graduating class. I help these graduates with their collars, fix their mortarboards, and wish them good luck.

Soon it is time to head down to the stadium to take my seat. I walk through the sprawling campus of enclosed hallways connected by outdoor corridors. The walls are mainly painted powder blue, the school's color. As I approach one of the outer gates, I inadvertently break up a drug deal as small packets of powder hurriedly exchange hands. The youth involved in the deal see me and quickly disperse.

Reaching the football field, I find a seat at the top of the rickety wooden bleachers in between a large group speaking Hindi and a Mexican family whose arms are overflowing with balloons and flowers for their graduate. Sitting alone I notice the many styles of clothing of the invitees, which vary from jeans and t-shirts, to one's best church clothes, to saris and dashikis. These colors combine with the signs, cameras, and many more bouquets of flowers and balloons of the crowd to create a kaleidoscope of colors and textures. At one corner of the crowd is a group of gang members dressed in red from head to toe, sporting red signs with the names of their graduates and the message "Class of 2000."

This diversity is fairly new for the school. In recent years, the bedroom community in which Whitman High School sits shifted from a primarily working- and middle-class area to a predominantly low-income and working-class town where 57% of families receive public assistance. This shift in population is particularly due to the dramatic increase (over 15%) of Latino immigrants who have newly arrived to the United States, causing local residents to now describe the town as a "minority majority community."

The bleachers are fairly full, but many seats still remain available. It is noisy, not only from the chatter of families speaking more than 20 languages but also from the screams of a host of crying babies and young children. Over half of the crowd chooses to stand, scattered across the football field. Many line up behind the podium, which has been protected from the crowd by a waist-high chain link fence.

Despite the mandate from the principal that all teachers be present for the event, only two-thirds or so of the faculty are present. Some line up around the stage, and others take their places at the end of each row of seats where the graduates will sit. Most seem to enjoy sharing this last moment with the graduates, although undoubtedly they have the role of keeping some of the more boisterous students in check.

Finally the nervous graduates file into the stadium in their powder blue gowns, and they take their seats in rows with teachers sitting on the edge of the aisles. Few distinctions identify the students as individuals, other than the broad range of skin tones, hairstyles, and scarves and cords draped around the necks of a select number of students to designate membership in school-sanctioned organizations, including the La Raza club, Adewole (an African American organization), and the school's honor society. An equal number of students are careful to have red peeking out from behind their gowns to signify their gang affiliation.

The ceremony begins as the graduates are seated. The young principal, new to the school this year, begins by tediously welcoming the crowd in each of the 15 predominant languages of the school. Rather than quieting down to hear him speak, the audience barely lowers its din to acknowledge the speaker. After the introduction, a small orchestra plays the national anthem and interludes between speeches, but the music can barely be heard above the din of the crowd.

Family and friends continue to arrive for the ceremony, which is already 45 minutes behind schedule. The audience reflects the diversity of cultures, ethnicities, and languages at Whitman. At the time of graduation, the demographics of Whitman were two-fifths Latino, one-sixth African American, and the remainder equal parts white, Asian, Filipino, and Pacific Islander.

Donald Goodwin, the vice president of the senior class and one of the students that I followed closely throughout the year, steps up to the microphone to speak on behalf of the graduating class. As the public address system continues to cut out on his voice, he shares his thankfulness of getting to graduation day and his praise to all of his classmates for remaining focused so that they too can share in this night. He talks about their desire to persist to graduate despite the distractions of their neighborhood. He explains how 400 graduates anxiously await their diplomas, only about half of the number of students who entered the ninth grade. Many of his classmates dropped out or transferred to transitional programs, and a few died from overdoses or gang violence. Says Donald, "Those of us sitting here are the students that kept getting up in the morning to come to school, who did their homework after coming home late from their after-school jobs, and who resisted the temptations of the outside world enough to earn this diploma."

An hour and many speeches later, each hard to follow due to the poor microphone equipment and crowd noise, the students file across the stage to receive their diplomas. Many of the graduates at Whitman are the first in their family to complete a high school education. Most politely shake hands and move along. Some stop on stage to make gestures of excitement, pride, or occasionally disrespect, on stage. Others return a wave to fans in the audience who have stood up to scream their appreciation for their accomplishments.

After the hats are thrown into the air, the crowd wanders down to the field to congratulate the graduates. While I came to cheer on many of the graduates, I particularly came to play the role of surrogate mom for Lata, a Punjabi graduate whom I came to know over the year and who was unsure if her parents would attend the ceremony. They do not speak English and did not feel comfortable coming to the public celebration. I snap pictures of her with her diploma and give her roses.

Lata and I walk among the now-graduated seniors, and I hand out flowers to other students whom I have come to know. I am struck by the intense emotions of the students as they say goodbye to one another. I sense much less relief and happiness than I remembered from my graduation day ten years before. Rather, apprehension and disbelief seem to be the predominant emotions. Most are sobbing, especially the boys, which I did not expect given their typical bravado. They clasp onto their friends, huddle in circles, and stare at each other. I reach over to hug one, and he tells me, "I never thought it would hit me like this."

It strikes me that this is an important ending for them, as with all high school students. But the notion of a commencement, a beginning, remains in question for many of them. Only a small portion of the graduating class will be attending college in the fall. Of the graduating seniors, only 20 percent go on to four-year universities, and approximately 40% attend two-year junior colleges. Most will switch their after-school jobs from part-time to full-time employment at McDonalds while they figure out what they will do next. Many others are joining the Armed Forces.

Despite the impersonal nature of their high school, Whitman was the community they came to know. They may not have always liked the school, but they came to understand its rules and grew to be a part of its culture. Leaving Whitman, many did not know what lay ahead and did not know which community they were entering, if any.

Whitman may seem an unlikely place for student voice to flourish. Its large population and transient student body reduce the possibility of building regular interaction, trust, and partnership building between students and teachers. Despite these potential roadblocks, Whitman stands among all the schools in the San Francisco Bay area as one of the few that has developed strong student voice in school reform.

The inspiration for student voice began with Whitman receiving a large grant from the Bay Area School Reform Collaborative (BASRC)—a $112 million education initiative that was supported by the Hewlett and Annenberg Foundations. This regional reform organization formed in 1995 for the purpose of sharing the lessons of school reform throughout the region. Eighty-seven schools received grants from BASRC of up to $150 per student for three to five years after completing a rigorous, evidence-based, peer-reviewed portfolio process. For Whitman, that amounted to $262,500 per year. The schools used the grants to fund support provider services, time for school inquiry and professional development, and other resources in support of their focused reform effort.

Rather than requiring schools to adopt a prescribed reform philosophy, BASRC entrusted schools with determining what needed to be improved and how. BASRC schools engaged in "inquiry-based reform," which is based on the belief that schools will continue down the present path unless reform processes are developed *within* schools (Cochran-Smith & Lytle, 1999; Fullan, 1993). Rather than importing solutions developed by outside organizations that presume to know how to fix schools, this line of thought suggests that teachers and administrators in schools possess unique knowledge about their schools' contexts. In inquiry-based reform, school personnel create their own research questions and take action based on their inquiry processes (Cochran-Smith & Lytle, 1999; Lieberman & Grolnick, 1996; Little, 1993; McLaughlin & Talbert, 2001). In other words, actors within schools examine their everyday realities to identify what needs to be fixed and how. They collect data from their schools, develop a vision of how they would like to change their schools, and then take steps to implement the vision. While such actions can be initiated at the classroom, grade, or departmental level, or can be school-wide, the intention is for the change process to become all encompassing so that critical decisions are driven by the newly developed vision.

As a part of their data collection, many BASRC schools sought information from students—a most basic form of student voice. Teachers analyzed student focus groups and surveys as part of the information used to decide how to proceed with the reform work (McLaughlin et al., 2000). Whitman chose a different path. Rather than having teachers interpret the data, groups of students at Whitman worked with an adult to analyze the focus group data of their peers. This work blossomed into students wanting to take action on the concerns that they identified in the focus group transcripts.

BUILDING CAPACITY FOR STUDENT VOICE

Like any change effort, student voice at Whitman did not occur in a vacuum. Whitman's path to student voice was paved with two visionary leaders whose work championing school change there created a context in which student voice could thrive. A charismatic principal—Patrick Firney—inspired the school to begin on the path of reform. Following a turbulent decade, which included a bitter strike, huge budget cuts, and the introduction of youth gangs to the area, Firney joined the school in 1995 and proved to be a dynamic leader who excelled at rallying the troops and keeping morale high.

Yet just as Whitman began with BASRC, Firney had to resign due to serious health problems. His exit caused a vacuum in formal administrative leadership. Over a year passed before a new principal could be found, and in this time some of Whitman's momentum for change began to slip. The district attempted to hire many candidates, but the high cost of living in the Bay Area, the district's low-paying administrator salaries, and Whitman's poor reputation caused many applicants to turn down the offers.

Throughout the continuous turnover in the formal leadership of the school, a guidance counselor carried the load of creating a new vision for the school. Sean Martin joined the Whitman staff in 1972. He began his tenure at the school as a teacher but quickly returned to graduate school to become a guidance counselor, a role he played for more than 20 years.

When Firney left, Sean took over the role of defining the vision of Whitman's future and the current reform efforts. A veteran teacher emphasized, "Although Sean would be too modest to say it, he's the one who galvanizes people. . . . And he's the one who people listen to, I think. If he didn't [direct the reform work], we would be up a creek—because he's the one who gets a vision and then gets other people involved in the vision—a long-range vision for reform at this school."

Combining the funds for this position and other sources, Sean gave up his guidance counselor responsibilities and began to work full-time as Whitman's "reform coordinator." Sean excelled in performing the delicate dance of communicating with all factions of the staff. He possessed the rare talent of knowing how to acknowledge the feelings of a diverse array of constituents and gaining the respect of the faculty. According to a veteran teacher, "He's got a way with people. . . . If something's not going right, he fixes it in a light way. When he's dealing with students and teachers, he always provides things so that they can get [problems] solved. He's got a lot of qualities of a very sensitive leader who knows how to get things done."

Sean's experience as a guidance counselor provided a strong base from which he could switch into the role of reform leader. He experienced the changes of the school firsthand over his many years of tenure. Yet during most of this time he was neither a teacher nor administrator, and he therefore did not carry the baggage of either of these camps during times of contention.

Sean's calming and encouraging presence was especially important when Whitman spent more than a year without an appointed principal. Even when Patrick Firney served as a powerful force at the school, Whitman relied on Sean's quiet skills to ensure that Firney's energy and enthusiasm turned into action.

Sean had a great ability to focus on the details of a plan. One teacher claimed in 1999 that the reform work would "grind to a stop" if Sean left.

Fitting with BASRC's focus on school-generated inquiry, Sean worked to enable the school staff to examine their everyday realities to identify what needed to be fixed and how. They created their own research questions, collected data, and attempted to take action based on their findings. Sean's specific responsibilities included creating action plans, developing staff trainings, and drafting budgets for spending the grant money and combining it with other sources of funding.

BEGINNING THE WORK WITH STUDENTS

Rather than requiring schools to adopt a prescribed reform philosophy, BASRC entrusted schools with determining what needed to be improved and how to use an inquiry process. Whitman decided to focus its reform on the question, "Why are so many ninth graders struggling to pass their classes? Whitman's plan to help ninth graders focused on using a large percentage of BASRC monies to buy time to create four ninth-grade support provider positions (NGSPs). Four teachers received a caseload of one-fourth of the freshman students (about 200 students) and one extra prep block daily of an hour and a half to conduct their work.

Initially the NGSPs treated their caseloads as a guidance counselor or social worker might. They chased after the students who seemed to be in trouble and did not have much time to attend to those who seemed to be on track. As NGSP Amy Jackson noted:

> Since the beginning of the year, the other Ninth Grade Support Providers and myself have set about the task of trying to figure out how we could best support freshmen. We tried a number of different strategies but found that much of our time was spent reacting rather than acting. We wanted to generate strategies of support that were sustainable so that when BASRC went away, support of freshmen would be ongoing. So now we're slowing down a bit, taking a more long-term approach, and trying to look deeper into the obstacles and types of assistance that can make or break a student's first year in high school.

Perhaps more firmly than anyone else at Whitman, Sean believed in the power of student participation. Prior to becoming reform coordinator, he quietly included students as a part of the reform projects on which he worked and also sought out students who would agree to mentor peers. Through BASRC funding and his new leadership position, Sean Martin had the opportunity to involve students more formally in Whitman's reform efforts.

The NGSPs and Sean decided to change the current system by having each NGSP assume the task of creating his or her own research project that would target a smaller portion of the ninth graders. The projects were intended to provide more support to the youth by learning from them.

One of the NGSPs developed a project to help understand the perspectives of the broad array of students at Whitman High School. Her project evolved into a strong example of a student voice initiative that helped both the youth involved and the school overall. Influenced in part by BASRC's emphasis on school-driven inquiry, fourth-year English teacher Amy Jackson developed a process for students to share their views on why students were failing at Whitman, to analyze the perspectives of themselves and their peers, and to decide collectively upon actions to take. As Amy explained in her letter to Sean Martin at the beginning of the process:

> Since students are what high school is all about, it only makes sense that they are involved in each step of the reform process. Over the course of the next few months, student focus groups will meet in order to think about what happens at Whitman during the freshman year and how we can help students to be more successful at this critical time of entry into high school. . . . Our hope is that by the end of this school year, our focus groups will have many new freshman support ideas which they will be ready to co-pilot as the class of 2003 enters Whitman next September.

Amy began this process by hosting student focus groups with the purpose of answering the question, What makes a successful freshman year? She designed the focus group questions to uncover what was not working for them in their classes and to learn from students what types of supports they needed to enable them to succeed. The focus groups reflected the diverse student body, including students representing a broad range of academic achievement and a variety of social cliques.

At the urging and with the support of Sean Martin, Amy worked *with* students to analyze the collected data. The students divided the data and worked in small groups in subsequent meetings to identify repeating themes in the focus group data. Amy, Sean, and two outside consultants offered assistance to each group by asking probing questions and providing informal assistance with research methods. The students particularly needed assistance with the process of breaking the data into chunks and generally organizing their work so that they accomplished the tasks identified as the joint work for each meeting. The adults also taught the students "education lingo," such as standards-based reform, to help them to identify themes in the data.

The students did their share of teaching as well, including translating student explanations into language that adults would understand. For example, in one focus group transcript the adults interpreted a student's comments as meaning that she did not see the value of coming to school. A student who was a part of the team analyzing the transcript explained to the adults in his group that this interpretation was incorrect. The student was missing school due to family problems. Yet when she came back to school, her teacher seemed very angry with her for missing so much class. Ashamed of the possibility of letting down her teacher and also mentally tired from the problems at home, this student did not want to engage in a confrontational situation with the teacher, so she stopped coming to class entirely. Through the process of reviewing the transcripts, youth and adults worked together to develop a common language and a set of skills that created a shared knowledge base from which the group could communicate and proceed with their activities.

Over the course of three months, the students and adults worked together to identify six main themes in the transcripts as the most pressing areas for reform at Whitman.

1. *Improved school reputation.* The students strongly believed that they attended a "ghetto school" and felt that the teachers, students, and broader community expressed this attitude. They did not want to feel ashamed of their school.

2. *Classes based on similar ideas/material.* Students wanted coherence in their education. For example, they expected that their 10th-grade math class would build upon the concepts learned in ninth grade.

3. *Better communication between staff and students.* Great animosity existed between teachers and students at Whitman. They strongly felt that this tension needed to be changed into positive relationships.

4. *Better/higher quality of teaching; higher standards.* Students wanted teachers to teach and to expect more of their students and to provide assistance so that students could achieve at high levels.

5. *Better counseling/more help planning for future.* Students felt that they did not receive sufficient support when making decisions about what to do after they graduated from Whitman. They wanted to know their options—such as attending college, finding a job, or enlisting in the Armed Forces—and they wanted to know the consequences of these choices.

6. *Orientation and preparation for incoming freshman.* Students did not feel prepared to enter high school and wished they had received more support knowing what to expect, including course selection and study habits.

The student focus group analysts presented their results to a regional conference on school reform and also to teachers in their own school.

Schools who received BASRC grants participated yearly at a Collaborative Assembly, an annual conference held at the end of the school year where participating schools shared promising practices and strategies from their reform work. Late in the afternoon, after an entire day of sessions, three Whitman students stood in the hallway in front of their meeting room. Joey, Sala, and Donald clamored for passers-by to come into their presentation as teachers and administrators scurried between sessions. More than forty teachers packed into the small room despite the fatigue felt by many at having attended several meetings and workshops already that day. Several of the audience members had been intrigued by the energy and enthusiasm of the hallway town criers and had chosen to skip the session that they had planned to attend to learn more about the work of these eager students.

When the room quieted down and the session was ready to begin, ten students were seated at a long table that faced the audience at the front of the room. Sean Martin and Amy Jackson introduced themselves and the students and then sat down to let the students run the show. The students reenacted their experiences in the focus groups by asking each other questions and giving their responses about what it is like to be a student at Whitman and what needs to be improved in the school. Then they explained the main themes that they had found in their data.

An air of excitement filled the room. Hands waved in the air as more and more of the audience wanted to ask questions of the students and to praise their work. The energy in the room was electric. When asked abut their future plans. Joey Sampson proudly responded, "Now that they've got us talking, we won't shut up!" Laughter rang throughout the room and the presentation ended with loud applause from the audience.

The presentation amplified the work of the group on many levels. The positive reaction of the conference participants validated the students' sense that they were engaging in something important. Rosalinda Gutierrez, a sociable, motherly Latina sophomore who struggled with her school work and preferred to spend her time working at Baskin-Robbins or hanging out with friends, later explained to me, "We told [the audience] what we were doing and where we wanted to go. . . . This program is for you—for us, the students—to get better programs, better teachers, more equipment for the school."

The presentation also helped to build students' collective identity. In particular, it helped to solidify for students that one of their chief roles in this group was telling what they knew about their school and expecting that others would listen because of the importance of their work. Donald Goodwin, the popular African American junior who would give the commencement speech the following year explained the value of the conference presentation. He felt that the audience needed to "know that students at this young age have an opinion. We know what we want and can see the different things that are happening. [We] let them know [about our concerns] in a respectful manner without raising our voice, getting upset and other ways that people have tried to do in the past, which have gone nowhere." Donald commented, "When I was talking to those teachers [at the conference], you could just see those eyes of people who just wanted to know what we were thinking. That just felt so powerful." Donald was an articulate, passionate student who did not have many opportunities in his life to have his self-worth reinforced. His mother was a drug addict, and many of his relatives were in jail. The conference presentation provided an opportunity for Donald to hear that people valued his perspectives.

Despite the positive response to their presentation, the focus group participants encountered some negative reactions to their growing belief in the importance and value of student voices influencing school reform—both at the conference and back at their school. In a large ballroom filled with tables of lunching conference goers, the students heard a speech by California State Superintendent Delaine Easton. Whitman students approached the microphone in the aisle and questioned Easton on the amount of student input provided on the state standards being developed. Easton responded that she did not believe that students were prepared to make decisions on what they should know—that such decisions should be left to adults. The Whitman contingent was shocked by her response. After several months of coming to believe that their voices mattered, the youth found it hard to swallow that one of the most powerful school officials in California believed that students did not have a place at the table. The encounter with Easton angered the youth and drew the group closer together as they began to identify what they were fighting against. The experience also helped to thicken their skins for their next encounter with their teachers.

Later on that month the focus group participants presented their findings about how to improve the school to Whitman teachers during a staff meeting at the end of the school year. Sophomore African American Troy Newman described the experience as it "let us know where certain teachers stood on certain things." Overall students and teachers who were present at the event viewed the response as positive. However, when students articulated their six concerns about the school and critiqued the lack of progress on these issues in recent years at Whitman, a few teachers began to get offended. Rosalinda Gutierrez explained:

> When we started talking about what teachers needed to improve in teaching, some teachers were very mean. They got offended. And I don't like that. I think that they . . . should take this as information in a positive way and not get mad or anything. They should say, "Well, you know, maybe I am strict, or maybe I'm not as friendly as I think I am." Because they started saying, "Oh, the students don't pay attention." Yeah, it's a lot of our fault, too. . . . But we think they should improve in this area and this area and this area, and they [should] actually do it. Like they say to us, "You should improve in this area—study more math or study more English." We don't get offended. . . . And they do.

If teachers could identify weaknesses in students, Rosalinda felt that students should be provided an opportunity to identify weaknesses in teachers as well.

The contrast in the span of a few weeks' time in the reception of their findings between the conference participants and the teachers at their own school upset the students. Yet these experiences also helped to solidify their vision of what they hoped to achieve by providing examples for them of what they were trying to push against in their work. Positive experiences encouraged the youth, and with the support of Amy and Sean, negative experiences helped to clarify what they wanted to change.

— ◆ —

Fast forward to BASRC's Collaborative Assembly two years later. Whitman students did not have to urge conference goers to attend their session. Word of mouth had spread, and teachers and students from other schools filled all the seats in the hotel ballroom. Others stood along the walls and sat on the floor to hear the students from Whitman speak about how they progressed with their efforts to increase student voice.

Joey Sampson, Troy Newman, and Marcus Penn began the session by discussing the group's efforts to share the focus group data with teachers. Joey began, "The main point is to figure out what is plaguing students and why they aren't doing so well in high school. A lot of us think it is because of the communication that's not happening with the teachers. And one teacher [when we shared our findings with them] was really avid that

'No, it's not the teachers, it's the students' fault. You guys are punks, we're right and there's nothing you can say about it.' And that's NOT what we're going for."

Troy interjected, "I just want to say that we don't want to point any fingers. We're together with teachers to fix the problems why students aren't learning the way we're supposed to." He turned to Marcus who added, "From last year, I think [that teacher] was trying to say that it should-n't just be the teachers trying to help the students, it should be the students, too, a half and half situation. That's what I got from what he said when we was making our presentation."

The crowd laughed as Joey retorted, "I guess that's what he was trying to come off as, but it didn't come out like that. It's hard to break down that barrier between student and teacher. A lot of times it's really hard to extinguish that and talk to them person to person. So that's proba-bly what he was coming off as and other people could have interpreted it that way [the way Marcus interpreted it], but I interpreted it as 'Me teacher, you student' and that kind of, I don't know, it wasn't good."

The negative experiences reminded Joey and other students of how youth were most often portrayed as part of the problem in high schools rather than part of the solution. Marcus felt that concerns from the teachers contributed to the work of the focus group by reinforcing the concept of the need for students and teachers to work together—and therefore that both students and teachers needed to accept responsibility for the problems in the school. The next two chapters document the work of Student Forum that took place between the first and second collaborative Assembly sessions—two years of struggles, learning, and ulti-mately many successful outcomes for the students and the school. All of these students in the group—regardless of their interactions with teachers—became inspired to continue to press for changes in student voice in their school. These experiences helped to solidify the interest of the group to commit to continuing the work of the group.

Chapter 4
DEVELOPING A VOICE

Based on their focus group findings presented at the first collaborative Assembly, the group members wanted to improve the school climate through better communication among faculty and students. They also wanted to increase continuity between classes and improve classroom instruction so that teachers held students to higher standards. Better counseling was another desire, both for entering students and those preparing to leave. With so many goals, it was difficult to decide how to choose a tangible focus for the next school year.

Student Forum began its work by holding an organizational meeting to rebuild common ground between group members. Some students who had participated in the focus groups had graduated, and other students were joining for the first time. The first meeting demonstrated the enthusiasm of the veteran students, but it also demonstrated a lack of purpose. The students knew that they wanted to increase their voice at Whitman, and they wanted to make a difference, but they struggled with what steps they should take to reach these goals.

On a balmy October afternoon during the last class period of the day, students slowly gathered in Whitman's roomy school library for the first Student Forum meeting of the year. Eight veterans from last year's focus groups greeted each other and asked how the new school year was going.

The students reflected the diversity of ethnicity, academic accomplishment, and cliques of Whitman High, each with stories of their own that would take more space and time than available here to do them justice. The veterans included Troy Newman—a shy, stocky African American junior—Lata Kumar—a first-generation immigrant from Punjab, India, who focused her energies on convincing her parents of the appropriateness of her going to college despite the doctrines of her Sikh upbringing—Erica Ruiz—a quiet, attractive Latina sophomore who struggled with balancing a very strict Jehovah's Witness upbringing with her increasing popularity at school—and sophomore Marcus Penn—a short-statured, wise-cracking African American who was deeply driven by his evangelical upbringing.

Students new to the group, mostly ninth graders, quietly took seats at the back tables and looked around pensively. Amy welcomed the group and asked junior Joey Sampson, another veteran, to begin the meeting by giving a history of the previous year. Joey, a scraggly self-described "skate-punk" who refused to categorize himself as any ethnicity, stood up and faced the assembled group. Prior to his involvement in the focus groups, Joey did not involve himself much with school. Due to Amy's encourage-ment, he was starting to join other activities as well, including joining the baseball team, and he became the stage manager for the school play.

Joey began his introduction of student voice by explaining the focus group process. He talked about how students shared their opinions, ana-lyzed their peers' responses, and combined them into themes. Amy wrote the themes on a flip chart as Joey was speaking.

Joey then explained the themes developed during last year's focus group to the new group members, reviewing and elaborating these themes, both to explain them and to get some laughs. "First is the issue of improving the school reputation," he told the group. "That might be a lost cause," he joked. He then moved on to the need to improve counseling in the school. "We need more help for the future. That may be a big thing because the counselors that we have are bogged down—three counselors for 1,840 students. So that's why they have you take that test for what you should do for your future. Counselors don't have time to listen to you talk!" He continued in a similar fashion, explaining what the group meant by the need for better communication between students and teachers, the need for standards and coherence between subject areas, and improving orienta-tion for ninth graders. While most of the veterans nodded approvingly as Joey continued, many of the ninth graders and other students new to the group appeared to be confused.

After Joey answered a few questions, Sean Martin explained the rationale for gathering and asked, "Why start with students? When we started last year, we got this pile of money and created Ninth-Grade Sup-port Providers like Ms. Jackson. We started the year just doing Band-Aid solutions. We decided if we were really going to make this work, we needed to take another approach. This project is Ms. Jackson's approach."

Amy wanted to develop a clearer sense of the group's purpose before the meeting ended, so she interjected, "We want to know what you think we should focus on this year. The way we do things is not about me and Mr. Martin deciding but instead about what the group wants to do. Definitely ask questions to get a feel for things. Look at the themes developed last spring. Is there a particular thing that you want to focus on?"

After Amy's explanation and encouragement of questions, students began asking about the group. From the questions, it was clear that the new students struggled with making sense of how this group was different from a typical high school club.

"Is this group going to be something recognized by the school?" asked Jaycee, a shy Latina girl.

While not directly answering the question, Amy took the opportunity to raise many of the issues she wanted the group to address, answering, "That's something we should talk about. And also how do we make this a permanent part of Whitman? How do we continue to involve students in big decisions and with changing the high school? What will we call ourselves so that everyone knows who you are? And who do we involve in this?"

Sala Jones then stepped up to the front of the room in an attempt also to answer the question, but mainly to share his view of the vision of the group and certain norms that needed to be established among its members. Sala was senior class president and commanded respect when he entered a room, even at the age of 17. He arrived late to the meeting after being hung up in a homecoming planning meeting, dressed in his standard attire—a leather letterman jacket proudly displaying his prowess in both football and track. Later on in the year a tenth-grade girl explained to me, "There are no 'popular' people at Whitman. Well, except for Sala." While his magnetism could allow him to intimidate others, instead he acted more as a coach and a cheerleader, trying to help his peers to "make it" in a school that tended to help most of its kids fail. Sala carefully thought about how to be a role model for other African American males, as his father encouraged him to do.

Sala turned to the students sitting at the tables and urged, "When participating in Student Forum, give an unbiased account of what you have to say. Try to enjoy this. We really are helping out the school. Help each other out too. Make this a nice growing experience. Like when I'm speaking you should all be nodding your head and saying, "Yes Sala, I'm with you." The veteran focus group members nodded their heads and agreed with Sala.

It was clear from the faces of the new students that the responses from Amy Jackson and Sala Jones confused them even further, because the descriptions did not fit with what they expected a school club to be. Hands timidly raised as more new group members asked questions. Bailey Clark was one of the newcomers who tried to gather the nerve to ask a question. Clark later explained that when he came to the first few meetings of the year, "I didn't really know what it was about. . . . I just came, and then, like I found out later. I thought it was required." Finally, Bailey raised his hand timidly and asked, "Will there be a yearbook picture? And do we have to do sales and stuff? Will we sell candy at lunch time?"

"We have a whole lot of money from BASRC. We won't have to do any fundraising!" replied Donald Goodwin, Sala's best friend as well as vice-president of the senior class. Donald's home life was filled with strife due to financial struggles and drug-addicted relatives, but school was a place where Donald could leave that all behind. He was known for charming adults and classmates alike with his sense of humor and generous smile, causing even thirty-year-old teachers to blush and giggle at some of his comments.

Sala, Donald, and Joey then together helped the group to pronounce the full name of BASRC, the funder for their group. "Come on, let's say it together—Bay Area School Re-form Col-lab-or-a-tive." The students just looked quizzically at the trio at the front of the room. The atmosphere in the room was not uneasy, though. The veterans clearly enjoyed each other's company and were glad to be back together. The new students seemed eager and interested, but definitely still confused.

Amy tried to bring the group back to the initial agenda: "I hear a lot of enthusiasm for spreading the word." To finish the meeting, Amy listed on chart paper at the front of the room:

Why do you think you're here?
What is Student Forum?
What should we hope to accomplish this year?

She then handed out papers for students write their answers to these questions. As new students filled out the sheets, the veteran Student Forum members quickly jotted their ideas down on the papers and then circulated to help others and answer questions. Amy and Sean opened bags of chips and bottles of soda. When students had stopped filling out the papers, they socialized until the end of the class period.

— ◆ —

This initial meeting illuminated issues that continued throughout the group's second year together. Questions were left unanswered, and both veteran students and adults seemed to struggle to articulate the group's purpose. On the one hand, the veteran students shared a commitment to improving relationships with teachers in the school and developing greater roles for students in the school reform process. Yet the dialogue in this first meeting suggested that the veterans still had trouble articulating to the newcomers (and to themselves) what these goals meant in practice and how to go about reaching them.

Joey talked through the themes for the group derived from the focus group analyses of the previous year—reputation, standards, counseling, ninth-grade orientation, instructional coherence, and improving teacher-student communication. Yet the concepts felt very large and vague when students tried to discuss them. In large part because the veterans had trouble articulating the group purpose, the new students assumed the group fit within the traditional frame of a student activity. Their questions focused on the common issues of fundraising, membership, and group recognition both inside the school and for future academic plans.

Unlike the previous spring in which the students focused on the specific task of participating in and analyzing focus groups, this year the purpose of the group was unclear. The group members had to decide what they were going to be and what they were going to do. What does student voice look like in practice? How is it different from a traditional student club? These fundamental questions took a year for the group to answer. To do so, the students needed to create an identity for the group and to develop a structure through which they could implement their vision of student voice. Key issues that the group had to answer included striking a balance between adults advising and youth leading the group, finding the time and space to come together to make decisions, and narrowing their vision to a workable action plan.

ADULT ADVISORS—LEADING WHILE GETTING OUT OF THE WAY

As advisors, Sean Martin and Amy Jackson engaged in "advisor angst," an ongoing, tenuous tap dance of trying to provide clarification of the group's purpose without imposing their own views of what the purpose of the group should be. Reflecting on the first meeting, Sean explained that he and Amy consciously struggled with trying not to slip into "teacher mode" and take over the conversation. Likewise, the students were used to the teachers taking control and expected it. Sean tried to pull the ideas and the progress forward out of the students rather than tell them how it should happen. In this first meeting of the year, Sean encouraged veteran students to facilitate the meeting, saying he only wanted to clarify when absolutely necessary.

Amy's guiding of the discussion—including the initial framing, the focusing questions throughout, and the wrap-up at the end—demonstrated her sense of obligation to keep the group on task. She and Sean steered the conversation in order to pull the meeting away from a focus on fundraising and recruiting to considering the purpose of the group. She too did not want to completely take control of the process, but even the veteran students were not ready to assume this responsibility yet. Throughout the year, Amy would work closely with students to learn how to facilitate meetings, stick to agendas, make decisions, and develop action plans so that their work could continue moving forward.

CREATING A STRUCTURE AND A PROCESS

Student Forum met monthly in Amy Jackson's classroom during the last class period of the day. To help enable students to assume leadership, Amy invited a small number of students to plan the group's monthly meetings. These planning meetings—what Amy referred to as the "planning of the planning"—consisted of informal gatherings in which Amy and a small group of students (whoever could get out of class to meet) would plan how to conduct the next large group meeting.

During these planning sessions, Amy engaged in several intentional efforts to make the planning more collaborative. She added several blank bullet points to the planning agenda to demonstrate to the group that she had prepared an agenda, but it was not complete.

In essence, Amy served the role of a coach rather than taking charge of the meeting. Amy admitted that she was used to being in charge, and the students were used to having an adult in charge. She debated whether to let students struggle and sometimes fail and how to coach without taking over. She lamented:

Oh, the frustrations of it all. . . . It's such a hard balance. . . . High
school teachers in general are very controlling. . . . It's a very different thing than teaching—this is definitely trying to step back while
also giving them some perspective when necessary. . . . But maybe
they're going in a way that seems totally frivolous or ridiculous, and
it's actually what really needs to be happening. It's so hard to know.
I want to get in there and tell them what's right, and it's really hard
to step back. I have to tie my hands under myself and tape my
mouth shut. . . . It's a fine line of learning how to foster, and
encourage, and also guide, to be a good coach and let it be what
they want it to be. You don't want to squelch it, but also, don't obvi-
ously want it to go wandering off in the cow pasture.

In part due to Amy's coaching and in part due to happen-
stance, students began to assume greater ownership on a rainy
February afternoon when Amy had to step away from the planning
meeting to speak with a colleague. Rather than the meeting stop-
ping as it might have just months before, the students pressed on
with the conversation and finished the group's work on their own.
Junior Donald Goodwin took over the job of facilitation, and the
group finished discussing the tasks to be covered during the big
meeting. One Student Forum member commented that the planning session format eventually allowed Amy to "hand the Student
Forum work to the students. . . . We have to do most of it, and it's
a lot of work—I didn't realize it was!"

Not only did the planning meetings encourage an increase
in student ownership, but they also provided opportunities for
newcomers to begin participating in some of the key decisions of
the group. For example, Troy Newman and Jill Bersola had
served very peripheral roles in the group and tended to sit on the
edges of the meeting until they attended a planning session,
which provided them the opportunity to voice their opinions and
to share in running the next whole-group meeting. Both students
continued to volunteer for responsibilities as time went on, to
raise questions and concerns when they felt the work of the
group was straying from its purpose, and overall to assume
important roles in the group. Without such opportunities to ask
questions and take risks sharing their ideas in a smaller venue, it
is doubtful that these two students would have developed the
sense of confidence and agency necessary to become influential
members of Student Forum.

CREATING A FOCUS FOR THE YEAR

Despite the progress that the group made in meeting structure and increasing the voice of many student members, the group still had not *done* much by the middle of the school year. Subcommittees continued to be rehashed every large group meeting, but few action steps were taken with any of the ideas. Amy and Sean urged the group to take some action. The students instead voiced a greater interest in broadening the numbers of students who participated in the group so that the collective was open and accessible to all. This tension between taking action and building up the membership of the group proved to be an ongoing issue throughout the year.

At the end of February, great shifts finally began to happen when those present during a planning meeting discussed the concern that not many students were participating in the meetings. As a way to amplify the voices of everyone at the meeting and as a way to get more work done, students decided to provide more opportunities for small-group work during the big meetings. During the next whole-group meeting, Amy told the group that they would work in small groups on three issues: "Some committees are on hold for a while, like 'supporting incoming ninth graders' because with too many committees we couldn't focus. . . . The idea today is to break into small groups and do some sharing, so we have more voices heard."

One of the small groups focused on increasing membership for the group. The subcommittee developed an activity to recruit new members, planned next steps, and even completed a task for their project by writing a letter to share with teachers. Perhaps it should have been expected that this last group would have the most success since it contained three veteran members, Joey, Donald, and Marcus, who had begun to develop a rapport and who had begun to develop leadership skills. It also contained Troy Newman, whose enthusiasm contributed to the positive tone in the group.

The concrete steps taken by the membership committee helped to propel their ideas into action. At the next planning meeting, membership recruitment became the chief focus of the group. As Troy Newman explained, "[W]e want to make student voice a part of Whitman High, a permanent part, not just something that came and went." Students translated this focus on sustainability into "spreading the word" and ensuring a broad participation of students in the future. The other committees discussed in the fall would wait until the next school year.

Similar conversations about sustaining the work and "getting the word out" could be heard in every formal and informal discussion for the rest of the school year. A discussion with several students and Amy during a planning meeting provides an example of developing this shared language as the group was brainstorming the goals for the spring:

> Joey: We're trying to pass the torch on.
> Jackie: That's a nice way of saying that!
> Amy: It's a way of making it a part of the Whitman culture and making it a natural part of the way that Whitman does business.
> Jaycee: We want to spread the word that [Student Forum] started this.
> Amy: So it's not only to recruit but that students know what Student Forum is and it's a place that they can go to.

The greatest benefit of the membership drive was that it forced Student Forum to be able to articulate who they were and what they planned to do. The group discussed possible questions that the students might ask the group, and the group tried to develop common answers to these questions. These discussions also led the group formally to choose a name for themselves. After a short debate, the group settled on the name *Student Forum* as best reflecting the group identity. Having a name became another source of pride and symbolism for the group. Student Forum members spoke their name whenever possible and identified themselves as the name—"We are Student Forum."

As a part of recruitment, Student Forum members also developed a mission statement to concisely articulate their vision. As explained by group member Sala Jones, "A mission statement. . . . explains what you are and what you are about and you can actually believe in. . . . This one really says perfectly what we are about." The students agreed on the following statement:

> Student Forum is an organization of students of all races and backgrounds at Whitman High School. By voicing our opinion, sharing

our experiences, and collaborating with students and teachers at Whitman and other schools, we seek to: help students become more successful; make education programs more effective; better Whitman's environment; and improve the reputation of Whitman.

The group members made copies of their mission statement, placed it in all teacher mailboxes, and asked them to please hang up the statement in their classrooms.

MEMBERSHIP CANVASSING

Student Forum members eventually decided to increase membership by canvassing the school the day before Spring Break. They planned to visit all rooms during third block to tell students about the group and to encourage their participation in it. Student Forum members practiced their presentation in front of the rest of the group as a way to provide feedback to each other and to share ideas for how to communicate their message effectively.

Finally, the day of the membership drive arrived. The students gathered in Amy's room for a brief pep talk by Amy and Sean. They received a short script of what to say prepared by students in the group and a stack of surveys to hand out to all students. The group split into pairs and divided up the classes in session to decide where each pair would speak. Each pair took responsibility for a portion of the classes in session during that time period.

One of these pairs was junior Troy Newman and freshman Bailey Clark. Bailey and Troy were given the task of visiting all of the classrooms in the new portable wing of the campus. Although Bailey and Troy did not provide the combination of one girl and one boy in each group as planned, they did fit the intention of one newcomer and one veteran, which the group had also hoped for when they planned for this day.

Despite his entrance into high school, Bailey could still easily pass for eleven years old. He often wore a scowl on his face, as if to provide a tough exterior despite his appearance. His English teacher recommended him to Amy as a potential member of Student Forum. She described him as a resilient kid with an extremely troubled home situation, yet he managed to remain focused and driven in school. He was enrolled in the few honors courses available at Whitman.

Over the course of the year, Bailey had grown in confidence about working in the group since the first meeting when he had asked why he was there. Yet the week before they canvassed the rooms, he expressed that he was just beginning to understand what Student Forum was about: "I didn't know what it was, like for about three meetings because we really didn't like do anything. But once we started planning for [the membership drive], it kind of got more obvious what we were about. And . . . I'll stick with it because it's a good program. I'm sure we're going to do something eventually.

Bailey and Troy decided to start their recruiting in the classroom of a teacher they both liked. Only a handful of students were in the room, and they were watching a video. The teacher paused the video, and Troy began his prepared speech, "Hi I'm Troy and I'm a junior at Whitman and this is Bailey, who is a freshman. We are a part of the group Student Forum." Troy then explained the work of the group, telling them that the group was about making changes in the school. He talked about the school's bad reputation and explained that Student Forum was trying to make changes in the school to improve Whitman's reputation by doing things like creating new courses and improving communication between teachers and students.

After Troy finished, he and Bailey handed out the surveys to students in the room. They patiently waited until the students completed the questions on the paper—Would you like to be a part of Student Forum? If so, why do you want to be a part of Student Forum? What do you think should be improved in the school? The students then collected the surveys and moved on to the next room.

As the presentations continued in classroom after classroom, Bailey and Troy gradually became more relaxed in front of the group. They ad-libbed and joked with each other, and Bailey became more comfortable doing some of the talking. Most of the students appeared indifferent to the presentation other than cheering for the interruption of their class. A few in each room listened intently and wrote long answers to the survey questions. Few students refused to fill out the survey.

Troy and Bailey finished their last assigned room with two minutes to spare before the class block. Expressing satisfaction for getting this task accomplished, they both rushed off to Amy's room to pick up their backpacks before their fourth block class.

— ◆ —

The membership drive activity offered the opportunity for students to work together. Troy assumed a new leadership role as a result of the activity and worked with Bailey so that he too could begin to share responsibility for their task. For both boys, the activity forced them to articulate the purpose of the group. Going to all of the classrooms also required them to identify themselves as members of the group and to serve as spokespeople for the group. Most important, perhaps, both boys expressed great satisfaction at the group successfully completing an activity for the first time that year.

Upon returning from Spring Break, three students summarized the survey results into a ten-page document, and Student Forum members read over the results. The most common problems expressed by Whitman students on the surveys were similar to those expressed by the focus groups the year before. Students expressed a desire for improved materials and facilities, more support from and better communication with teachers, and more engaging classes. Additionally, 137 students expressed an interest in joining the group. The large number of interested students left the group scratching their heads about how to accommodate all of this enthusiasm.

SPRING: REFLECTION ON THE YEAR AND PLANNING FOR THE FUTURE

With just one and a half months of school remaining, Student Forum did not have time to develop another project from the goals they established at the beginning of the year. Although they talked about working on increasing Advanced Placement courses in the school, researching the development of a homeroom period, and building communication between teachers and students, their membership drive represented the one significant activity of the year.

A pressing issue facing the group before the school year ended, however, was how to build off of the membership drive and to ensure the sustainability of Student Forum for the following year. Based on feedback from the conference, Amy and Sean felt that they needed to become more assertive in presenting the direction of the group in the last meeting, or the year would end without plans in place for the next fall.

During the final big meeting of the year, Amy told the group: "We only have two and half weeks of school left. So how are you going to harness those 137 people [who want to join]? . . . We don't know what to do with them. . . . We need a process to figure out substance." Rather than taking the time to develop many options and develop a consensus on the best future structure for the group, Amy felt the need to act fast. Rather than continuing their style of scaffolding the students' work with questions, they inserted some ideas into the mix to ensure that a structure for the next year was put into place. With two weeks left in the school year, she felt that there was simply not enough time to have smaller planning meetings and to prepare students to assume roles in this decision, particularly since she could not pull students out of class again because finals were quickly approaching.

Based on an idea that Sala Jones suggested previously, Amy suggested that a core group of five to seven "Student Organizers" could meet with Amy the next year as a class. The students would be responsible for attending to the day to day responsibilities of Student Forum, including planning group meetings and communicating with administrators. The Organizers could get credit through the school as "teaching assistants." The rest of the group would continue to meet monthly during and outside school hours as it had this year. The twenty students present at the meeting expressed appreciation for the structure and thought it was a good way to proceed.

This last meeting of the year ended with a call for action from Sala Jones, one of the graduating seniors, who told the group: "This group has been going on for a year and a half now. . . . Maybe next year is about taking the action so students know what it is we're really doing. You'll be really organized with the structure so maybe that could happen—the action!" For Student Forum, the best was yet to come.

Chapter 5

TAKING ACTION AND LEADING THE WAY

For the first large group meeting of the next year, students slowly filter into Amy Jackson's classroom. The tables are lined in rows, and Student Form members find seats. The Organizers stand in the front of the room, off to one side. As rain starts to fall on the window panes during this chilly November afternoon, Student Organizer Jill Bersola writes the focus for the year on the board. To begin the meeting she welcomes everyone and reads the sentence to the group: "Our focus is to build partnerships with staff at Whitman."

The Organizers want to begin the meeting by stressing their role in the larger group in a nonthreatening way. Yet they also want to share ideas that they have developed and honed through meeting as a class for the past two months.

Jill moves to the side, and Joey hollers out, "Now Marcus is going to say what student voice is. It isn't a club. It's not about being members. We want everyone to come with us. He'll explain how we're a system."

Marcus steps to the front of the room and says, "Even though we're joking around, this is really serious. We want to make a student voice system so they have to hear our point of view, so we can build up a relationship between teachers and students, therefore creating a better school. Therefore, it isn't all teachers deciding this. It will also be students, and creating a better relationship with teachers and having teachers get a better understanding of what we think and what we want to learn."

Joey interjects, "We want to build a better learning environment so you guys aren't butting heads with teachers."

The other Organizers stand up and join Joey in front of the group. Felipe, a newcomer to the group whom Amy urged to join as an Organizer, adds, "The six of us, we're the organizers—the ones who put every thing together, and we tell you guys what we're doing."

Felipe turns to Rosalinda and nudges her. Rosalinda looks at the group and explains," We use the metaphor we're the legs, you are the ears and the brain. We want your input on matters. The six of us can't do everything. So we're the ones that organize and make these meetings happen, but you're going to be a part of everything that goes on We need you guys to get involved."

Joey concludes the first agenda item, by stating, "That pretty much sums it up. We're here for you guys. We do the legwork and get stuff done, and you tell us what the students want. We listen to you. We can only do so much alone."

During the second year of Student Forum, Student Forum Organizers met with Amy every day as a class. By creating a system in which students could work together every day, the six Organizers pushed Student Forum beyond its inertia and made progress toward its vision of increasing student voice and reforming the school. The Organizers assumed responsibility for the ongoing responsibilities, including planning agendas for upcoming meetings, delivering permission slips to excuse Student Forum members from classes, writing letters to teachers to inform them of upcoming events, and contacting other schools in the area.

Student Forum still met once a month to learn about the ongoing activities of the Organizers, to sign up for specific activities, and to deliberate on current and future plans. Thirty to fifty students attended these meetings. Student Organizer Jill Bersola explained the role of the broader membership as a source for "gathering information. . . . I don't think we're the authority or anything, but we offer them tasks to do to be part of this. . . . We give information to them, and they just take a role in what we want them to do." While the daily Organizer meetings provided opportunities to engage more deeply in the group's activities, the large group discussions provided a time to impart information to the broader membership with information, to seek input, to answer clarifying questions, and to recruit people for specific tasks.

The Organizers felt that they needed to establish a tone from the first large meeting that they were not usurping control of Student Forum but instead doing the legwork that the broader group could not accomplish by meeting once a month. Aware that there might be some hostility toward them, the Organizers tried to stress from the first large group meeting that they did not want to usurp the authority of the entire group. Yet, by default of meeting every day and spending so much time working on group activities, they ultimately guided the group throughout the year in the decisions that it made.

None of the members raised concerns about the group structure. Rather, they appreciated that they were moving forward to take some action. Meeting every day and building on experience from previous years in Student Forum, the Organizers developed the capacity to engage in some decision making on their own. Jill Bersola explained:

> The main difference this year is that we're doing more action. Like last year all we did was talk. It was good because we were gathering up information for this year. But we kept talking. . . . And it's going much quicker than last year. Because [last year] we would meet one meeting a month. And the meetings would be so far between. Right now we have a more intimate relationship with the program, and we can do more.

The Organizers saw all of the planning and capacity building of the previous year leading into the actions that they were planning.

ADVISING YOUTH LEADERS

With students meeting every day to work on Student Forum projects, Amy could assume much more of the coaching role that she preferred and had to do less of the actual work herself. A discussion of three of the Organizers explained this shift in Amy's role:

Joey: Before, [Ms. Jackson] had to do all the work. . . . And now we have taken over . . . not really taken over, but assumed the role similar to hers. And then, like, she's backed off a little bit more.

Rosalinda: Because she's seen us grow and knows that we are dependable.

Lana: That we can handle it.

Rosalinda: Yeah, we can handle pressure. We've just grown to a certain point that we can take care of things. But not necessarily have her be behind us, you know, and say, "Did you do this? Did you do that?" She knows we're going to get everything done. [Last] year, we went to meetings, and we listened, and she was doing all that we are doing now. Now we have more power, and we have more knowledge about what needs to be done.

The Organizers felt that Amy pushed them beyond their current frames of thinking and helped them to realize the next steps that the group needed to take. One Organizer explained that Amy was always stressing to them, "Remember you've got to be a little more professional. It's the little things that count."

Increased student leadership did not eliminate the advisor angst of how to best support youth, but instead it raised new questions regarding how to counsel the group most effectively. While initially students needed more help, the Organizers became more skilled and felt confident not to rely on Amy as much. Lana explained, "She means very well. But sometimes an advisor needs to learn how to let go sometimes. . . . Let the students do what they need to do. Because we learn by our mistakes." For instance, Amy tried to demonstrate to them the standards for working with adults. This emphasis on producing quality work was appreciated by the students. Yet unlike the previous year in which perhaps Amy could have helped a bit more, the Organizers felt that Amy helped too much. Amy particularly struggled with when to prevent errors that could cause the group to look unprofessional. "So I always edit them," she explained, "Especially if they're going to staff. And the kids feel squelched [when I do]."

The tension between enabling the Organizers and getting out of their way proved stressful for Amy. She needed advice and encouragement as much as the students did. Amy's experiences fit with research that has indicated that teachers need to be empowered themselves in order to empower others (Bauch & Goldring, 1998; Muncey & McQuillan, 1991). During these difficult times, Sean often served the role of mentor and sounding board for her. Sean's 30 years of experience in the school district as a guidance counselor gave him a broad perspective on working with youth. His support of Amy involved listening to her concerns, serving as a sounding board for ideas, and helping to advise the group about political strategy and school context. Sean explained, "What I've been trying to do is make sure I'm there every day . . . , trying to be a buffer, but also to try to really help so that she doesn't just get totally frustrated."

Sean also provided a source of inspiration and energy for the group. When Amy felt like she was struggling to keep the group going, Sean would remind her of all the group's accomplishments. Amy emphasized, "On the day-to-day it will feel like we're crawling, getting nowhere. And he'll come all pumped up and [say], 'I'm just amazed at what we've accomplished this year!'" His praise and broad-based perspective kept Amy and the students motivated to continue engaging in the tough work of change.

NARROWING THE FOCUS

The creation of the Organizer class allowed Student Forum the time and human resources needed to develop a vision and move forward on activities to achieve it. Student Organizer Lana Marcos explained how the vision for the year was developed: "We sat down [as Organizers] and thought about what is wrong in the school, and we wrote down different things. We went to classrooms and asked students. We picked the main ones they mentioned and whittled it down to one." Fitting with the initial focus group themes from spring 1999 and the feedback that the group received from Whitman students during the membership the previous spring, Joey suggested that Student Forum hone its focus on "building partnerships and communication between teachers and students."

All the Organizers agreed this school climate issue was one of the most pressing ones and one that they could tangibly tackle. Student Organizer Rosalinda Gutierrez explained that the focus was "having teachers actually understand students, and students understand where teachers are coming from. A teacher has to push a student no matter what kind of situation they are in or where they're from. And students [have to] believe that no matter where they come from they can do the same good job as the person sitting next to them." Through building stronger connections between students and teachers, the group emphasized equity for students.

The Organizers spent two weeks seeking feedback from teachers and students on how to go about enacting this vision of greater understanding and partnership between teachers and students. Rather than specific suggestions for what to do, the students expressed their concern that the teachers did not relate to them as individuals. The teachers also indicated an interest in learning the perspective of students. Marcus explained that when they talked to the teachers to get feedback on increasing communication, "a lot of teachers wanted to see more personal, seeing through students' eyes."

Student Forum developed two complementary strategies for building communication between students and teachers that can be classified as "student-focused" activities and "teacher-focused" activities. Student Forum developed student-focused activities in which the group helped teachers to gain a better understanding of student perspectives. Through neighborhood tours and forums on school reputation, they urged teachers to expand their current perceptions of their students, the school, and their own practice. In teacher-focused activities, students joined in the reform work that teachers were conducting, such as participating in staff trainings and research groups on reform. As youth participated in these activities, they gained a greater understanding of the perspectives of teachers and of how the school operates. By developing this two-pronged strategy, both teachers and students taught each other about their perspectives, and both learned to be open to the other's point of view.

Student-Focused Activity 1: Neighborhood Tours

Tying together the desire of the students to be understood and teacher interest in learning more about their students, the Organizers decided to focus their energies on developing a student-led tour of the surrounding neighborhood so that teachers could see where they lived. The Organizers carefully made preparations for the student-led tour. They surveyed the teachers to determine the best possible day and time for the activity. They advertised the tour and gathered a rough count of the teachers interested in attending. They also offered a training session so that all Student Forum members could serve as tour guides, complete with worksheets and maps of the area that the tour guides could use to prepare their routes. One of the most important aspects of the training was the establishment of norms for the car rides. For example, they decided that the radio should remain off, that students and teachers should stagger themselves so that all of the teachers were not in the front seat and all students in back.

On the day of the student-led tours, participating teachers and students meet together in Amy's classroom after school. Amy and the Organizers divide the 30 participating teachers and 32 Student Forum members into groups small enough to fit into the teachers' cars. They also hand out maps of the area and the norms and guidelines sheet.

Groups head out to the parking lot to begin the tour. I join two young teachers from the math department and Student Forum members Marcus Penn and Jaycee Garcia. Marcus has been a part of Student Forum since the first focus groups. He takes the train to school from about half an hour away, so he is not familiar with the local area. Jaycee, on the other hand, lives right around the corner form the school, so she takes charge of the tour route.

She first directs the group to a local nonprofit community center, La Familia. Jaycee enters the building with nonchalance, suggesting that she belongs here. It is clear when we walk in the building that Jaycee is a familiar face. The secretaries at the front desk warmly greet her in Spanish. La Familia is located in a fairly run down building, but it is filled with an atmosphere of compassion and safety. The colorful signs and charts on the walls provide an indication of the commitment of the staff to providing support, education, and opportunity to the Latino community.

Jaycee begins the tour by taking us in to meet the director of the center, a jovial Latino man whose office is filled with plaques and other tokens of recognition for his ongoing dedication to the community. He provides us with a brief explanation of the many services offered by La Familia to the Latino community, including youth leadership programs, food drives, parent education opportunities, and community building events.

The Whitman teachers remark that they did not even know that such a thriving community organization existed just blocks away from Whitman. They trade contact information with the director and make promises to meet again to think of ways that the school can collaborate with the center in the future.

Jaycee then shows us around the facility. She proudly shows the offices of the youth leadership center—a place where she spends most of her afternoons. She explains that she gets paid through a small grant that the director acquired. As we are leaving, Jaycee points out the toys sitting by the door and says that she is currently involved in a toy drive in preparation for the upcoming holidays. I make a note to drop some gifts off the following week.

After leaving La Familia, the conversation in the car indicates the excitement that we all feel after visiting the center. We spent over 45 minutes touring La Familia, but Jaycee suggests that we visit the local community park before returning to the school. One of La Familia's projects has been to clean up the park and to strategize ways to ensure that it is a safe place for children and adults to enjoy. She notes the new play structures, pavilions and indoor community room and discusses how she participated in fundraising and how La Familia's directors worked hard with local officials to ensure that more lighting would be added to keep it well lit at night time. She also explained that police officers would increase patrols of the area. Jaycee views the park as one of the greatest successes of La Familia's community involvement efforts.

After walking around the park, we get in the car and return to Whitman's parking lot. On the drive back, the teachers ask about Jaycee's experience taking night classes at the local community college. She is taking classes to catch up with her credit hours since she had struggled with some subjects at Whitman the year before. Jaycee responds that just the night before she was followed home by some older students who eventually grabbed her purse. She expresses some concern about going back to class again since she will need to walk home again. The two teachers sit with her in the car in Whitman's parking lot and discuss ways to help her with her problem. While they do not come to a definitive solution, Jaycee shows appreciation for having the opportunity to share her fears and their efforts to help her strategize a way to keep attending her evening class.

Jaycee had been a member of Student Forum for over a year now, but before this tour, I had never seen her assume a leadership role in the group. She had always been a quiet participant in school activities. It was clear from her tour of at La Familia, however, that she is greatly respected in her own community and that she had many skills to share at school as well. Marcus described Jaycee's tour of La Familia as, "It was really a heart feeling, really touching. I was learning too. Jaycee told us how they work to make the world better. They go around the area they live in and survey different houses to see how people felt about their neighbors. La Familia also helps students to solve their conflicts. It was really cool." The tour provided an opportunity to show talents that we never knew about before.

Due to careful planning and reflection, the tour proved to be a huge success for all of the groups. In the words of one student tour guide, "It was cool. They [teachers] learned where we lived, worked, the different territories, where we stay away from, where people get killed and hurt for being in the wrong areas. I thought it was really successful."

Some students were surprised at how little the teachers knew about the area around the school. Even the principal had never explored much of the community. A guide who went with the principal's group remarked, "I was in the car with the principal, and we took him right down the street. We got fifty yards away, and he got lost. Now he knows where I live. And I see him down the hall, and he says hi to me. He'll go out of his way. I've seen a lot more of the teachers try to make an effort to say hi and include students in their conversations." The experience of the tour helped to form a lasting trust between this student and the principal.

More than one-third of Whitman's 90 teachers participated and responded enthusiastically about their experience. All told, both teachers and students expressed great satisfaction in the opportunity that the tour provided to build deeper relationships between teachers and students. In the words of one teacher who reflected on the day, "I think you guys inspire us." Students also expressed that they truly did come to know their teachers better, and the teachers came to understand them more as well. One Student Forum member reflected, "I learned a lot about the teachers, [maybe even] more than they learned about me. I look at them different now." The tour proved so successful, in fact, that the administration decided to make the tour a regular part of new-teacher orientation each year.

Student-Focused Activity 2: Ghetto Forums

As a second student-focused activity, the group wanted to address the school's reputation—a pressing concern that was raised during the first days of the focus groups. By creating opportunities to openly engage in a discussion of labels, Student Forum members encouraged their peers to discuss their identities and what sources they draw upon to define that identity. They hoped that by raising consciousness about the different interpretations of individuals and their neighborhoods, they could create a collective sense of the direction in which they wanted the school to move. Student

Organizer Joey Sampson explained, "Ghetto is an important topic because we're classified as 'ghetto'—our school is. And the neighborhoods that we come from are. We were like, 'Well, our reputation is that we're perceived as a ghetto school. So it's like where does that come from?' We wanted to deal with that directly." The topic caused such an emotional reaction on behalf of students that even efforts to plan the ghetto conversations—both among Organizers and in the larger Student Forum meetings—caused side conversations with students debating what their impressions were of whether Whitman was ghetto, if such a reputation was embraced by the school and surrounding community, and the implications of these views.

The group decided to initiate the conversation with the broader school by hosting student discussions on the issue, which they called "Ghetto Forums." The group sought student input on this question through two venues. The first was an open microphone during lunchtime in the quad. They also facilitated a more structured discussion with the school's Legislative Assembly, a group of students elected to represent each homeroom in the school.

Through the discussions, Student Forum learned that students used the term "ghetto" as a source of identification and pride among their peers but viewed it as derogatory when used by people who did not live in their neighborhood. Joey Sampson reported how the students felt about the term: "I don't think that people like being called 'ghetto.' I think it's kind of like taking the power back. You know, like, no one likes to be classified as ghetto. But you've got to have pride for where you come from! I've got to be proud of it because it's where I grew up, and this is where your memories are from."

Other students viewed "ghetto" as a state of mind that lowered expectations for themselves and for others. One example of the reaction of a senior African American girl was:

> If we were in a rich area, and people didn't live up to the expectations of their grades, then they'd have low self-esteem. We are in an urban area [with] diversity, [so] then we're considered ghetto. People have these subtitles based on where you live or your ethnicity and we play into that, and we do that all the time. If we feel less than, then we are less than.

As the next step in the process, Student Forum facilitated a similar conversation with all of Whitman's teachers during a staff development day. The staff broke into nine groups, each of which had a student and a staff member as cofacilitators. Similar to the student Ghetto Forum the teacher groups discussed what "ghetto" meant to them, how it applied to Whitman, and the consequences for the school. Student Forum later shared these teachers' perceptions with students who participated in the first Ghetto Forum.

Student Forum member Terrell Jones observed that the teachers seemed to have a different opinion of the concept of 'ghetto' than students. The teachers felt that students used the term to excuse themselves from aspiring to higher goals. Terrell reflected, "The teachers use 'ghetto' to lower our expectations. They think we use it as an excuse."

Senior Student Organizer Lana replied, "So how do you get them to change their perspective or get students to change their perspectives?" The group planned to continue these dialogues the next school year and to think about how to move beyond the stalemate that existed based on differing perceptions about students and their neighborhood.

The discussions in essence forced the school to address one of the taboo issues in the school, which opened up an avenue for talking about race, class, and discrimination. Amy explained the importance of the issue to the school: "The reputation of the school and the attitudes of the students are intimately related to how well [students] work with their staff. [Having conversations about the school's ghetto reputation] just kind of blows me away in fact because a few years ago I would have never thought that possible."

Sean viewed these discussions as crucial if Whitman was to push beyond mediocrity and make great improvements in student performance and school climate. He therefore created time for the staff to continue to think about the issue in the future. He hired 20 students to participate in Whitman's two-week summer institute (paying them $200 each), both to work on teacher-student relations and to give teachers feedback on assessment development. He explained that as a part of the school's summer institute, "we're setting time aside for what we call 'Whitman Issues,' and the primary issue is this issue around teacher expectations based on perceptions of students and what that means and how that plays out in a classroom." By continuing to have students and teachers work side-by-side, Sean, Amy, and Student Forum members hoped that the school would continue to move forward on improving communication.

PARTICIPATING IN TEACHER REFORM

In addition to designing student-focused activities, Student Forum engaged in many teacher-focused activities. Amy and Sean encouraged Student Forum to participate in school reform work as a way to share their viewpoints and to help influence school policies. The students agreed and chose to invest a great deal of time engaging in teacher-focused activities. They participated in many professional development and training sessions with teachers.

The first day of three-day professional development training begins at nine in the morning on a balmy August day. Whitman teachers sit six or seven in a group at tables in the school's library. Shelves of books surround the cluster of tables, and a row of floor-to-ceiling windows at the back of the room provides cheerful light. About one-third of the school's teachers are present (25 out of 80 teachers).

Ten students also join the group. Sean greets them and asks them to sit two to a table so that they are evenly distributed about the room. A clipboard is passed around, and all of those attending sign in for the meeting. All of those attending, including students, will be paid for their attendance at this training session.

While waiting for the meeting to get started, I speak with Pedro, a short-statured math teacher with a thick beard and mustache, who has been teaching at the school since 1972. He talks about the shift in the student population and comments that he found the youth much more respectful years ago. With a soft-spoken, earnest demeanor, he whispers that students today need a lot more nurturing and need to be given space. His tone seems concerned but a bit weary from the challenges of his current students.

Half an hour after the meeting is scheduled to begin, Sean Martin begins the day by welcoming everyone to the meeting. He stands in front of the group, in about the same place as he and Amy and the Student Forum veterans did at the first Student Forum meeting. Sean explains that this professional development day is about creating meaning from the written state standards and asking what kinds of assessments to use to get to standards. A main focus will be on the links between standards and teaching and learning. Next to him stands Sharon, an outside educational consultant and former teacher.

Sean then introduces the students at the meeting. He emphasizes that the students are "partners in the conversation. We are on a journey, and the students here are partners in the journey. This is not a hierarchical relationship but a partnership of equality." Sean also stresses the importance of students and teachers keeping specific names out of the conversation when they were offering a critique of a teacher's practice or a student's behavior and experience. In mixed company, he explained, the naming of individual people could create problems.

As a warm-up exercise, Sean passes out sheets of paper and asks everyone present to jot down notes about "what your influences are and how you got to your role at Whitman." Everyone bows their head and begins jotting down ideas. Sean roams the room and consults with students to see if they are comfortable with the activities and understand the work.

A teacher expresses concerns with his ability to do the assignment. Sharon explains that their work on standards is going to build on everyone's existing philosophy, "so I want to connect them with what everyone feels and everyone thinks" rather than people feeling that what they currently do has to be left behind.

Once a low murmuring begins in the room, Sean asks the tables to share what they have written. At one table, Ann, a warm and friendly heavy-set English teacher speaks first. She talks about learning from her exhusband who was Mexican and the concepts of diversity that he taught her. The sharing continues around the circle. Peter, a history teacher, talks about being influenced by social justice and the lack of the American dream. Carrie, sporting a Berkley sweatshirt, discusses her powerful experiences in college and her commitment to reaching all students. Sharon, the facilitator, joins the group and adds that her greatest motivation was a student who gave her a withdrawal slip along with her term paper.

Lata, a serious Sikh student whose family immigrated from India to escape persecution, speaks next. Looking down at her sheet, her first words written are "great grandma." She quietly talks of how her grandparents still send her all of her clothes to wear in the United States, except for blue jeans. She says that she wrote about her experiences moving to the United States, including leaving friends and family and learning to "deal with problems alone." She also talks fondly of taking summer classes at the local community college in precalculus and biology to allow her to begin the college preparatory track this fall in school.

At the end of the sharing, Sharon compliments the group members on the intensity of task. She then transitions them into the next activity. She tells them, "We all say that all students can learn. Last year there was concern and debate for English as a Second Language (ESL) students, who are 40% of Whitman students, as to whether they all could actually keep up with the standards that the school was affirming. When developing your assessments, you need to make sure that you are assessing the standards and not their understanding of English. A specific example is the [school's exit exam]. A test question required knowledge of American culture— "What is a touchdown?" So the assessment did not assess their analogies ability but their awareness of culture.

Andrea turns to the group and asks students in the room about their experiences in sheltered classes (more than two-thirds of the students present are Latino.) Elsa, a quiet and studious senior, raises her hand and explains, "We've talked about having students translate the directions in Spanish. ESL students don't know what's happening in the classes. It's easier for them to have other students explain to them, so peer tutoring and translation would help them."

Jack, the shop teacher, offers, "About the communication, in a shop class over a three-year period, I've had two occasions of students who spoke no English. We worked up a deal with another student in the room that bridged the gap. In one case the student was pretty successful. It may not be as appropriate for another class but it worked for me."

Sophomore Anita Lozano comments, "Often the teacher is not patient enough to repeat what he or she has said in shelter class. [We] don't get it quick, so [we] don't do our homework. You said it too fast, and [we] didn't catch it."

Peter, an English teacher, comments, "I try to say the only dumb question is one that's not asked. I had a sheltered class for the first time last year. The epitome of understanding happened for me during a vocabulary lesson. The student said, 'Mr. Hoffman, we'll never understand if you use words to define the vocabulary that we don't know.' It's on the student to say when they don't understand. If they don't say you don't understand, how can I as a teacher know? If we ask you, and you don't respond, there's an assumption that you do."

Social studies teacher Kara Lopez interjects, "I almost [entirely] agree with you. I'm for personal responsibility for students. Before that you demand that of a student, you have to foster a climate in our classroom where students don't feel comfortable to ask questions. Unless you spend quality time making that a priority in your classroom, you can't expect students to feel comfortable to say they don't understand. They need to be sure you'll respond well to their question."

Sean adds, "One of my lenses is how does the system respond? We moved to a block schedule that included 20 minutes of office hours, but we haven't really achieved that. Maybe we need to remind students that those office hours are really there. That's a contractual negotiable item that is part of our collective bargaining agreement. That's a beautiful place to work one on one with students. I would encourage you as [teacher] leaders to promote that. In some places that won't be popular, but when you accept that responsibility you should honor it."

Joey Sampson replies, "Sometimes it's not the teacher creating the environment and feeling comfortable, but it's the other students in the class. I can tell there are other students in the class who don't understand. They're afraid to raise their hand and look dumb."

Peter queries, "Does class size matter?"

Joey responds, "Yes. And block scheduling allows you to feel comfortable with people in half of the year. If there are less people than 32 or 34 people, you're more inclined to speak and say what you have to say."

Alison adds, "Climate in the classroom is crucial, it sounds like most people are saying." She talks about trying to say happy birthday in many languages during her class. Seeing her struggle and take risks allowed her students to do so as well.

Sean tells the group that it's time to break for lunch. The BASRC funding, in addition to paying for the training, pays for lunch. The teachers and students react with enthusiasm and appreciation when they learn this.

During lunch, I ask Lata if she likes participating in the training session, and she replies, "Yes because the teachers listen to what I say."

After the break, Sean then explains to the group that the students had a pretraining the day before. He used the day to explain to the students the activities that would be happening at the meeting and to learn some of the educational vocabulary that they would be hearing through the day, such as standards-based units, assessments, and curriculum.

Sean also taught the students about multiple intelligences and worked with them on how to articulate the ways in which they learn best. He had the students engage in exercises in which they discovered whether they learn better hearing a lesson, seeing it, or engaging in an activity. Sean explains, "Certain cultures will emphasize one type of intelligence over another [equity], and I know I'm preaching to the choir on this, but sometimes we forget. I would suggest that it is something you might want to give to your students at the beginning of the year is having students go around [and] share their best and worst intelligences."

Sean turns to Sharon to explain how the students would be able to use this newly acquired knowledge to explain to teachers what types of instruction would allow them to learn better. Sharon explains, "Since we have student experts at each table, we're going to ask students what their most powerful learning experience has been." Sharon provides her own example of her experience in a self-defense class. What mattered in her learning experience was that she was coached. The application of learning was immediate, and the teacher believed in her. She then asks the group to begin the activity.

At one table, Anita explains that she had difficulty in her class because "the teacher was not teaching the way that I learn." A teacher questions whether always giving students choices may mean they do not improve upon their weakest skills. Anita responds that she needed other ways of seeing things to learn better. She comments, "In my honors U.S. history class, I was overwhelmed by all of the information. During the pop quiz, I got a D. And I never get Ds. I told the teacher, 'I needed some tutoring!' Right after school, the teacher spent two and a half hours with me, including showing me pictures, cycles, and everything. She allowed me to keep the worksheet with the examples. I studied it, and it was a great description of everything. The pictures and chart [were] much more helpful to me. I needed the visual learning. This experience showed me my weaknesses and strengths. I got an A on the test the next day. I was so happy."

Jess, an English teacher, asks, "So what has this taught you about when you leave us and go on to college? Sounds like you need visual, hands-on, and one-on-one instruction."

Anita nods, "Yes, I need to see it physically."

Rod, a new math teacher, asks, "If the teachers would have shown you the pictures in the class, would you have gotten it?

Anita, responds, "Yes, but one on one she was concentrating on me. I felt comfortable because I didn't want to speak out that I didn't get it. Other kids wanted to move on. I never had a teacher who sat with me in history especially and explain everything in detail. I never had a teacher do that for me in math."

Jess reflects, "In a group and others are tired and bored. She doesn't want to hold everyone up. There's peer pressure."

Sharon stops the conversations and asks the whole group to share what they have learned.

One teacher comments, "Julio told us about the importance of relating material back to their life."

Jess adds, "Access to one on one tutoring with our teachers so that they can work specifically on what you need."

Ron nods and adds, "Lots of visuals, graphs, tables, and pictures."

Other teachers add other reflections, including the following:

"When you already have a relationship of respect with our teachers."

"When you can extract the knowledge you used in multiple incidence— transference of skills outside of the classroom."

"When you can learn things on your own and when you are able to ask for help."

"Making mistakes and learning through life experiences."

"Honest, caring teachers who want you to succeed."

"Our two students told us that they valued real, emotional experiences of satisfaction or intensity. An affective component is important."

— ◆ —

This professional development day demonstrated ways in which students were used as resources for improving teacher practice. In activities such as the ones described above, teachers drew on students' knowledge to reflect on successful and problematic teaching strategies. In other sessions during the three-day training, teachers and students were asked to pair to try out practice assessments and to connect statewide curricular standards with their lesson plans.

The teachers also taught students as well throughout the training session by checking student understanding of what was happening. Along with Sean Martin, many teachers conferenced with the youth to see how they were experiencing the day and what questions or feedback they had on the activities. At times, a teacher would even lean over to a student and "translate" a discussion from teacher-speak to everyday language. The more discussions became frustrating or passionate, though, the fewer teachers remembered to actively include students. At these times, Sean encouraged participation by asking for student comments.

Student Forum contributed to the teachers' reform work in other ways as well. For example, the group improved the school-wide writing assessment that all students took twice a year to measure writing competency. After learning that students did not take the assessment seriously because they did not see its relevance to their lives, Student Forum suggested that they develop the questions for the assessment for the following year so that the topics would be relevant to students and phrase them in language that the students could understand.

To develop good essay questions, Lana explained, "We went out to the classrooms and asked students what issues they wanted to write about. And now we're taking them and trying to write the prompts about things [that] we think the students would have no trouble writing on." Organizer Jill Bersola suggested that students also cograde the assessments with a teacher. The grading took place on a student holiday, however, and the group could not get enough student volunteers to help with that part of the project.

ADDING STUDENT VOICES TO THE TEXTBOOK ADOPTION PROCESS

During the second semester of the school year, Student Forum Organizers lobbied to become a part of another teacher process that previously did not include student participation or input—choosing textbooks for Whitman courses. Students particularly expressed frustration about the math curriculum at Whitman, College Preparatory Math (CPM). The students felt that the textbooks did not provide them with sufficient examples or explanation. The Student Organizers decided to address this problem by eliciting large-group feedback on student experiences in math classes.

During a large-group Student Forum meeting in February, Joey and Marcus stand at the front of Amy Jackson's classroom. Marcus looks out at the students casually sprawled out behind the rows of tables and writes on the board the letters CPM.

Joey begins the meeting by explaining that many comments from the student survey last spring expressed criticism of the school's math curriculum. He asks for feedback on ways to address this pressing concern.

Monique: I don't like CPM. In classes with CPM we fail or come out with a low grade.

Joey: We don't want to turn this into let's bash CPM. We know, so what do we want to do about it?

Jill: Maybe we can compromise with math teachers, like having the option of CPM or teacher-led.

Joey: In CPM, I can't just read it and get it. I have to have some people teach it to me. Some teachers assume that if you're in a high-level math you should be able to catch onto it.

Tenisha: Teachers aren't as involved as they should be.

Marcus: We need to think of solutions to this problem.

Janet: The teacher has to want to be involved. It has to be something that the teacher is willing to do.

Jerome: Basically CPM is a math book without examples. You can't just blame it on the teachers and the book. You have to want to make an effort, too. Not exactly putting examples in the book, but the way to help is to make the book more specific, the problems more to the point where everyone can understand.

Shawn: We need to get away from the bashing of the CPM and get your input about getting the teachers to come to talk about it.

Joey: This isn't a CPM math bashing time.

Jill: I think it's a really good idea to invite them because we can get a better idea to learn about CPM and get that third perspective.

Marcus: So that we can give them our input about CPM.

Shawn: We can convince them to change the CPM style.

Marcus: So we are having the meeting or not?

Group members nod their heads, and the Organizers promised to arrange a meeting with the math department.

— ◆ —

Student Forum hosted a meeting with the math department during the next large group meeting. Through dialogue with teachers, the math department agreed to include student recommendations as a part of its final decision-making process. Sean Martin explained the importance of involving students in the textbook selection process, "We're considered by the state to be an underperforming high school, so part of our strategies are to solve issues of numeracy. This will involve discussions between staff and students, and hopefully these will be a precursor of what will continue on so that we don't get back to [teachers reverting to old ways]. There's ongoing accountability by Student Forum with these teachers."

To provide input into the process, the Organizers created an evaluation form that Student Forum members could use to rate potential textbooks at the next large meeting:

Math Book Survey

Grade_____   Book # _____

Please read each question. Look at the book, and circle number (1–4) that best shows your response to each question. 1 is strongly disagree; 4 is strongly agree

Would this book work for all grades, cultures, and genders?

1   2   3   4

Are the word problems in the book understandable? Do they refer to real life situations you can relate to?

1   2   3   4

Would this book appeal to students with different styles of learning?

1   2   3   4

Could you use or learn from this book on your own?

1   2   3   4

Does this book have clear and specific explanations to the problems?

1   2   3   4

How do you feel about CPM?

1   2   3   4

Any other overall comments about this book?

During the Student Forum meeting, group members critiqued all of the possible new textbooks and identified which books seemed to provide the best explanations and which appeared confusing and unhelpful. After tallying the evaluation forms, Student Forum members recommended two textbooks that they believed would best meet the needs of Whitman students based on criteria such as whether the book had clear and specific explanations to the problems.

Much to their disappointment, they learned that as they were engaging in their own evaluations, the math department had already chosen their text. The district had placed strong pressure on the department to choose the book that the other schools in the district had chosen, both to reduce the price of the book order and to help create a uniform curriculum across the district. Although the students were pleased with the textbook that the math department chose, they were greatly disappointed that they were not included as part of the process. The Organizers felt that they had been led to believe that they were a part of the decision-making process, but in fact they were not.

— ◆ —

To address the concerns felt by the Student Organizers about the lack of receptivity to student input on the textbook decision, Sean arrives at Amy's classroom to speak with the Organizers during their regular class time, shortly after their negative experience with the math department. The students are not working on student voice activities that day. After hearing the day before that their efforts to provide input on the textbook adoptions were thwarted, she could tell the group needed a break from their Organizer responsibilities. Instead, they are doing their homework, talking to their friends, and listening to music on their headphones.

Sean greets the group and asks the students to move the desks into a circle. The students quietly do so. Joey reluctantly joins the group after much cajoling. Of all of the Organizers, he is the most disappointed about how the textbook adoption effort failed. When Joey finally takes his seat, he looks at Sean and asks, "Why do this? They didn't listen to us. We filled out the surveys, but they went forward without talking to us. They already knew what they were going to do, so why fill out the surveys? We were all really upset about it."

After a pregnant pause while he looks into the eyes of each Organizer, Sean replies, "I got a slightly different impression than that. The math department chair said that she took the questionnaire with her to the district meeting." Sean continues, explaining to the group how the school board works. He discusses how some items on the agenda are open for debate and some are part of the consent calendar, where they vote yea or nay without any discussion.

The Organizers start discussing whether maybe they should go to a school board meeting to express their concerns about the lack of ability to provide input into the textbook process. Sean suggests that the group get on the school board agenda in order to present the research that the group has conducted on math text books.

Amy asks Sean and the others, "If they really like the book being chosen, why present comments in favor of it?" Amy's comment reflects her shared disappointment and frustration about the recent events.

"To set a precedent for future textbook adoptions." Sean replies. He looks at the two-page district guidelines for textbook adoption that he has brought with him. He continues, "These guidelines are all very 'adult worded.' The goal is to set a precedent to have student voices heard." After another long pause, Sean looks into the faces of students and asks, "So what does it mean to be Student Organizers?"

Joey retorts, "I don't know, to organize things?"

Sean calmly continues, "Part of organizing students is to be proactive."

Student Organizer Kristina Sampson follows along with Amy's thought pattern and asks again, "If they like the book, okay, we agree. So what's the point of going to the meeting again?"

Joey softens his tone and begins to assume some leadership in the discussion. He replies to the Organizers, "I guess it's not so much about this incident, but I guess we need to say, 'You need to listen to us; we give this consent.' We want an active role."

Amy nods and adds, "Part of your presentation wouldn't be 'We give this consent' but that students want to enter themselves into the conversation. And maybe it's easier for the first encounter to be positive."

Joey continues, "Rather than 'We're students and we say no,' we give our consent."

Sean nods his head as well and explains, "The consent is based on what criteria you developed for the surveys. You want to demonstrate the quality of the work you did. The bell is about to ring. I want you all to think about if this is something you want to put your energy into or not. We've heard from two voices today—Joey's and Kristina's. What do the rest of you have to say?

Kary replies, "I think it's good to put in our input even if we say we like it."

Shawn nods his head and says, "I agree."

Amy then interjects, "Another idea is to focus our energies on the next textbook adoption here on campus. What about the science department? They will have their textbook adoption next year. Maybe we should be proactive and ask if we can be invited to their initial discussions to see how they're thinking about it? So that it's partnership and not adversarial?"

Sean replies, "That's another way to focus your concerns. So next steps. There's too much adult talk in the textbook adoption process. We need to change that. I talked today more than I usually care to. Adults should model partnership. But I was concerned about how you felt the process went. Tomorrow, you all need to discuss how you want to proceed with this initiative—go to the school board, focus on the science textbook adoption next year, or another strategy."

The bell rings and the students gather their books and head to their next class.

— ◆ —

Sean demonstrated in this conversation his role of trying to keep the focus on the broader vision of student voice rather than on one failure of the group. He tried to boost the spirits of both the students and Amy. He wanted to show to them the value of the work they had done and to encourage them to continue to be involved in the process. Most of all, he wanted to provide a space in which the group members could vent their frustrations and feel that they were being heard about this important issue.

Over the course of the following week, the Organizers decided that since the math textbook decision was already made, they would focus their energies on other activities on which they were working. They believed that they had gotten involved in this adoption round too late, and they planned to become involved in the science department text adoption from the beginning.

After some time to dampen the frustration they had felt, they began to look forward to the next adoption as an opportunity to use the lessons they had learned from their first experience. Student Organizer Shawn Brown explained, "The first textbook adoption, it didn't go as we planned. They already had a book, and we kind of got in, I guess, too late. We didn't really have no say in none of that stuff. But we got the jump on it now. We're going to be in everything next year for the science department." Although their immediate experience in the textbook adoption process proved to be one of the low moments for the group, the Organizers felt positive that their hard work that spring had taught them how to become involved in a more meaningful way in the future.

BUILDING BRIDGES

Student Forum members learned over time that the change process is slow and of the need for developing patience and relationships with those in power. One Organizer summed up the value of building bridges by stating, "[To be heard] you have to have power so that you can get stuff done. Power is buy-in from teachers and students. For us to have power, we have to be recognized by the staff. . . . We also have to have student buy-in because they need to show that they want this power and that they can also handle it if they're given it. The student body needs to have faith that what we're doing is right for them."

Throughout the year, the Organizers developed an awareness of the time it takes to create that meaningful change and an appreciation for the modest victories as they tackled greater challenges. "This whole thing takes time . . . [;] it's not about immediate results," Amy explained. In the past students expressed frustration about how slow things were moving. This awareness of the patience that it takes to make changes within the school indicated a shift in understanding from the previous year.

One way to build support for the group's work was to develop communication with various power sources in the school and to communicate successes to the student body. Amy explained that the group needed to "know where the power lies and where you need to go for it."

One key connection the students made was establishing biweekly meetings with Principal Juan Mendez. The purpose of the meetings was to keep the principal informed of the group's activities to ensure his support and to learn more about his main goals and concerns for the school. During their first meeting with the principal, the Organizers asked him to walk through the same list of questions that the students had discussed during one of their ice-breakers as a way to get to know him. Rosalinda explained, "The principal went through the questionnaire so that we would be able to address him on a personal level. So it wouldn't be all businesslike.

We have meetings with Mr. Mendez whenever I can schedule in a day with him. And it's like he comes to *us* and meets us. And, like, you don't hear about that happening much. Overall the group found him to be supportive of their work. We don't see him around our campus a lot. But every other week he sits in our classroom and talks to us. He's an advocate, I think, for the most part."

Amy and Sean found it particularly important to keep dialogue open with Juan because he did not think there needed to be a distinction between Student Forum and the school's Student Council. Amy explained, "I know that Juan sees the two as one. And I think he'd like to see Student Council become a little bit more political. . . . But I think it's Student Forum that models and takes on the political role to whatever extent is possible. We check in with Student Council to make sure we're not overstepping our bounds. We try to leave doors open." Amy explained that she did not feel that Student Forum was being threatened by Juan: "The biggest threat is that there's so many things on the plate financially that need to be taken care of." As long as outside funding from BASRC and other sources continued to support Student Forum, it did not run the risk of being compromised for other priorities in the school's at-large budget. Continuous communication with Juan helped to secure Student Forum's position in the school.

To build a bridge with the Student Council, the Organizers became actively involved in the school's new Legislative Assembly, which was a representative body of students from each classroom. Although the Student Council developed the process and organized the elections, eventually Student Forum designed the content of the meetings.

The Legislative Assembly became a new way for the Organizers to publicize what they were working on and to gain broader perspectives of the school. At the first meeting of the Legislative Assembly, for example, the Organizers told the group about Student Forum and asked the assembly representatives to explain to their classroom constituents what Student Forum was so that the whole school would hear about it. While the Student Council was responsible for school facilities issues and extracurricular activities, such as buildings and grounds, clubs, dances, and school spirit activities, the Organizers emphasized that Student Forum could address concerns related to teaching and learning and school policy. Student Organizer Felipe explained, "They're more into the social things, and we're more into the political things. But we're trying to find a way to bond with them."

LOOKING AHEAD

The support for student voice and the successful activities built upon each other to increase momentum for the group and to help them to think about potential actions and activities for the following year. Rosalinda felt that Student Forum was slowly building the capacity to make changes. She explained, "We started on a rocky road. I guess we were disorganized. But we got more knowledge, and we knew how to answer to people who are not responding to us as we would like. [We learned] to be calm and have patience and see that hard work does pay off at the end. Now they can see that we *are* doing something. It might be baby steps to get to the main goal, but in the long run we do have a lot of power to communicate with people." The other Organizers nodded their heads in agreement as Rosalinda shared this observation. Amy, Sean, and the Student Organizers began to indicate their desire to push their agenda a bit harder in the future.

Milbrey McLaughlin (1993) uses the term "visible victories" in her research on leadership opportunities for youth in after-school programs as a way to indicate the importance of finding a way to boost morale through successful activities, especially when the group has worked on making difficult changes in its community. The "visible victories" that Student Forum experienced created an energy and confidence among all Student Forum members. Joey felt that with the momentum Student Forum could assume an even larger role in making changes in the school. He commented:

> People are starting to be receptive to us and want to help us out. We just had a meeting with the vice principal about the problems that we're having with the bathrooms. And then the next day, all the bathrooms were completely clean, and they were open, and, like, the stuff was getting fixed. And it's like I've heard a bunch of people lately just be like, "Man, did you see that both the bathrooms were open?" And people are having Forums with staff during staff days. And we have students in the Reading Research groups, and the staff is stoked about that. We've got buy-in from them. We've also got student buy-in because it's us working every day to get this done. And then we've got the big Student Forum meetings, where they

come in and we pull information from them and they're stoked about getting stuff done too. And I think that's what makes Student Voice powerful here. We're starting to get buy-in.

Student Forum members were starting to see themselves as change agents in their school.

The broader membership felt more empowered as the year went on as well. At the beginning of the year the members sat quietly and listened to the Organizers. By the final Student Form meeting of the year, the overall noise of the room was much louder as members engaged in conversations with those around them about the issues at hand. The Student Organizers reflected on the meeting the following day:

Kristina: Student Forum has grown since the beginning of the year. There's a lot more people at the meetings. And people . . . used to come [and] just sit there. And now . . . the same people that used to sit there are now saying stuff. There's a lot more action going on.

Lana: More issues are picking up. More things we're saying we want to change and trying to get done. More people are being interested. The word's getting out more. Stuff is getting done, so people are getting more interested, saying, "Okay, something is happening."

Rosalinda: They want to give us their ideas, their opinions. [At] our last meeting it was almost overwhelming. They were so excited to participate and share. They were having all these little individual conversations. But it wasn't about, like, "Oh, what did you do last night?" It was about school issues. And it's just a big difference since the beginning.

As Student Forum looked toward the future, the Organizers and Amy talked about needing to gain a stronger understanding of the obstacles preventing their work in the school and where the sources of power are and how to influence them if they were to preserve the work of Student Forum for years to come.

— ◆ —

At the end of the year, the Organizers gathered together for an end-of-the-year party to sign each other's yearbooks, munch on food, and reflect on the work that they had done. After the bell rang to excuse them from their class for the last time, they lingered, saying goodbye to each other and exchanging hugs. Similar to the role that Sala played the previous year, Joey expressed a desire to be able to return and see the group continue to thrive. He explained:

> I watched all of student voice happen from when we all were in focus groups three years ago when seniors were sophomores. We don't want the work that everyone has done to flounder after this. I want to come back and say. "Hey I helped to start this" and we all want to be stronger for next year.

The group members nodded their heads and left the room together.

Chapter 6
MAKING A DIFFERENCE AT WHITMAN

The experiences of Whitman High School raise important questions for how schools can broaden current conceptions of a school's learning community and decision-making processes. As mentioned in chapter 2, *professional collaboration* has been shown to lead to improved teaching and learning as teachers work together to critique practice, to support professional growth, and to learn together how to improve practice (Grossman, Wineburg, & Woolworth, 2001; Leonard & Leonard, 2001; Lieberman & Wood, 2001; Louis & Kruse, 1995; McLaughlin & Talbert, 2001; Newmann, King, & Youngs, 2001; Talbert, 1995). Such learning communities can improve individual teacher practice and build the collective capacity of teachers (Little, 2003). To foster a collaborative environment, communities need to cultivate environments that encourage the sharing and processing of information (Brown & Duguid, 2000; Little, 1993). Key strategies for encouraging thriving learning communities include establishing a baseline trust (Achinstein, 2002; Friend & Cook, 2000; Leonard & Leonard, 2001; Westheimer, 1998), intentionally creating a democratic community that includes meaningful roles and shared responsibility and decision making among participants (Copeland, 2003; Friend & Cook, 2000; Little, 1982; McLaughlin, 1993; Senge, 1994), and providing learning opportunities for group members to develop the capacity to be able to assume meaningful roles (Fullan, 2001; Leonard & Leonard, 2001; Stokes, 2001). Most discussions of collaboration in schools have focused on teachers collaborating at the grade level or departmental level or teachers and administrators sharing decision-making authority on schoolwide decisions. This chapter broadens the definition of collaboration to include students as members of school-based learning communities.

Student Forum invested enormous energy and effort to improve the climate and academic outcomes of their school. In the process, it sought to establish the legitimacy of student voice as a crucial part of school change activities. A survey of all Whitman teachers conducted at the end of this research (Center for Research on the Context of Teaching, 2002) found that 85% of teachers at Whitman indicated that they felt the school had seen an increase when asked about student voice in school decisions. Many (23%) even noted a "substantial increase," the highest level of change they could indicate. An increase in student voice was the greatest change noted by Whitman teachers during the tenure of their BASRC grant—greater than changes in curriculum, school structures, leadership, professional development, and parent involvement issues.

These survey findings indicate that Student Forum had begun to influence conceptions of student roles in the school. By emphasizing a partnership between students and teachers, Student Forum sought to build support for its initiatives and to gain respect and responsibility from teachers and administrators. The group believed that changing student outcomes required changing the culture of the school, and changing the culture of the school required an increase in respect and understanding between students and teachers. Their "teacher-focused" and "student-focused" activities provided important initial steps toward establishing the credibility of students to contribute to school reform. Table 1 summarizes Student Forum's efforts to establish a learning community that is based upon collaboration between youth and adults. Students provided classroom expertise during professional develop-

Table 1. Teacher-focused and Student-focused Activities

Teacher-focused activities	• Participation in teacher professional development and staff meetings • Action research groups on reading strategies • Schoolwide writing assessment • Textbook adoption
Student-focused activities	• Initial sharing of focus group data with faculty • Student-led tours of neighborhood • Ghetto Forums

ment sessions, motivated adults to persist in their struggles to improve classroom practice and school climate, and bridged teacher and student perspectives to show the common desire to improve teaching and learning at Whitman and to develop strategies to accomplish this goal.

Through these teacher-focused and student-focused activities, which were detailed in previous chapters, Student Forum's school-based youth-adult partnership created conditions that helped to strengthen teacher practice and to improve climate conditions in the school. The remainder of this section will elaborate on these conditions. Specifically, Student Forum provided pedagogical feedback, inspired and motivated adults to persist in working toward change at Whitman, and worked to bridge teacher and student perspectives

Providing Pedagogical Feedback. Through participation in teacher professional development sessions and reading research groups, Student Forum members became valuable members of the school's learning community by providing teachers with feedback on how students might receive new instructional strategies and materials. Student Forum member Troy Newman recalled, "One teacher asked me how do I feel about teachers and who are we comfortable with. And I told him that a teacher who is kind of laid back and kind of . . . gives you kind of freedom. . . . And learning about something as you're going through something." Student participation in teacher-focused activities offered information for Whitman's reform effort that otherwise could not have been provided.

Student Forum members served a second role as translators between teacher and student experience. In addition to explaining student responses in the focus groups, Student Forum members also helped teachers to translate their words into language that students would understand. A Student Forum member explained that his role at the meetings was "breaking down vocabulary. Some students may not understand, you know. So we were trying to put it [the rubrics and the departmental standards] in a way where all students understand. I guess you could say [I was] a translator." Troy helped the teachers change language from teacher-speak to student-speak.

In addition to the benefits of improving the school change effort, the students also benefited directly from learning about the types of changes that the teachers were trying to make. For example, participation in reading research groups helped students to gain a greater understanding of pedagogy and curriculum. A student participant explained, "One of the things that [teachers in the group learned to use was] reading circles. My teacher used it on us today [in class]. Knowing where it came from, having the background, that was cool knowing what we were going to be doing." The student's participation in the reading research group helped to improve her own learning and to gain a greater understanding of the classroom from a teacher's perspective.

Inspiring and Motivating Adults to Persist. Beyond providing a specific source of knowledge, teachers mentioned that having students present at this and other staff meetings helped people to stay on task and reminded them of the purpose of the meeting. One teacher explained:

> It focused them on the reason we're here. And a lot of staff remarked just how you get a really sometimes surprising, sometimes a very insightful perspective with a student at the table, and you don't have to second-guess what they would think. Because so many teachers seem to think . . . they often think they're the experts of how students would react and what they would think. And I think people find it refreshing. And a little intimidating for some people to have them there, but I've heard positive comments.

Student Forum kept teachers attention on the reason for persisting with making changes, despite the difficulties of engaging in such challenging work. Teachers noticed the difference when students were present. Student Forum's participation in meetings helped to improve the productivity of the reform-minded faculty. It also reduced the apathy and hostility of resistant teachers, who were less likely to engage in unprofessional behaviors such as completing crossword puzzles during staff meetings or openly showing hostility to colleagues.

Students noticed this shift in tenor as well. Joey Sampson commented, "When teachers are with each other, they're with their peers. But with students around, their teacher part engages, and they want to show that they can be on task." In essence, the youth served as an accountability mechanism during teacher meetings. The students provide a gentle form of pressure to keep teachers focused and collegial.

In addition to these meetings, Student Forum's work inspired some teachers to partner with students to make changes in classroom pedagogy, to continue to involve students as they returned to their classrooms to implement what they had learned. An outside consultant who worked with many teachers at Whitman and other schools on designing curricular units explained:

> The teaching assistants [students who get class credit for assisting a teacher] ended up doing some more of the reform work. I mean, I ended up sitting down with Julia and her teaching assistant (TA), and we unpacked her assessment and put a rubric together. The same with Henry and his TA, and also with a couple of science teachers, Margaret and Jessica and their TAs. It was interesting in that it's really clear at Whitman that students support teachers, and we all work together.

The consultant observed that Whitman was unique among the schools that she coached. Although they worked on similar reform issues, and the consultant encouraged other schools to follow Whitman's example and include students more actively in changing classroom practice, none of the schools chose to do so.

Bridging Teacher and Student Perspectives. Student Forum members observed an increasing willingness to collaborate with students and to engage in dialogues and a deeper growth in teacher understanding and receptiveness. During their initial dialogues with teachers when they presented their focus group data, students discouragingly observed that a few teachers reacted in an openly defensive and hostile manner to their presentations. Over time, however, Student Forum members observed an increasing willingness to collaborate with students and to engage in dialogues and a deeper growth in teacher understanding and receptiveness. Over time, the students began to feel a part of the school's learning community. Through multiple interactions, students and teachers recognized that they had similar reactions to activities.

The neighborhood tour and the Ghetto Forums in particular helped to amplify the message of expanding the *distributed leadership* of the school (Elmore, 2000; Lashway, 2003) as students had the opportunity to teach their instructors and administrators about their community. The activity made further gains as well by helping to reduce tension between teachers and students, to increase informality, and to help teacher and students to identify one another as individuals rather than as stereotypes. For example, one Student Forum member commented that in her tour group, "Teachers and students learned equally. We got off track talking about our lives in general instead of talking about the neighborhood. I felt like I was driving around with my friends. There was no tension." Given the history of tension between teachers and students at Whitman, students and teachers alike appeared to value the opportunities to build positive relationships.

Students emphasized that they came to understand the teachers, and they believed that the teachers came to understand them as well. Joey Sampson, one of the few Student Forum members who had been involved in the group since its inception, commented, "For the most part, I see the teachers as more receptive to the students now . . . They look at students a little bit differently. And I think students look at teachers a little bit differently. That's our main goal. Teachers need to know that students do have a voice, and students need to be listened to." Joey found that the teachers appeared to value the opinions of students and, when necessary, even agreed to disagree without becoming hostile about their differences.

Sean Martin also noted a change in teacher-student communication during the Ghetto Forum activity that occurred later in the same school year. He commented,

> It's fascinating what [students] were saying about how teachers responded to them—a lot less condescension! One young man was saying, "I never thought I would agree with that teacher!" And really feeling much more of an equal basis. . . . So we're going forward with a better relationship between students and staff. We noticed a real difference, and I think some of the students did too. [There was] tons of praise for the students who helped facilitate the Ghetto Forum discussions. [Teachers] thought it really connected to what they wanted to see happen. It was a huge step forward.

Overall these strategies of providing feedback—motivating adults to continue and bridging teacher and student perspectives—strengthened Whitman's fledgling professional learning community. Indeed, in a school where teachers did not have a tight community themselves, in many instances the students brought them together to help them focus on their practice and to learn how to work together as colleagues.

PROCESS MATTERS AS MUCH AS PRODUCT IN STUDENT VOICE

Inevitably, however, school contexts greatly influence the type of influence a group can have (McLaughlin & Talbert, 1993). Change does not happen in a vacuum. Rather, organizational contexts can enable or hamper change efforts. Despite the large roadblocks created by the starkly differentialized roles for teachers and students in schools, the experiences of Student Forum suggests that creating collaborative youth-adult partnerships is possible and that student voice can help to strengthen teacher learning communities as well. In particular, the activities at Whitman High School offer key lessons in the types of supports that enabled student voice: the creation of norms to ensure a balance of power, the need for a strong adult advocate, the support of those in power, and the establishment of sustainable structures that allow a group to continue to work on a regular and purposeful basis.

Norms to Ensure a Power Balance among Group Members. One important strategy for moving Student Forum from ambivalence to partnership was that the group paid careful attention to group process, and in particular the power balance between adults and youth. Student Forum intentionally developed common norms (participation, caring, inclusiveness, and shared leadership). It also created a group vision, which first became articulated through a group mission statement, and continued to become more clearly defined as group members engaged in activities that they believed to be meaningful to their goals of increasing student voice and improving their school.

Adult Advocate. Amy increased her colleagues' support of Student Forums' work through conversations with them at departmental meetings and at the copy machine. Through constantly looking for opportunities to champion Student Forum's work, she sought to build bridges between Student Forum and other reform efforts happening in the school. She also sought to buffer the group from potential concerns or conflicts that might put a stop to Student Forum's agenda. These efforts align well with research that suggests that organizations use two strategies to manage their task environments: actions that buffer the core focus of an organization and actions that bridge the boundaries between one's organization and partners, competitors, and superiors (Scott, 1998).

Amy possessed a strong commitment to the idea of student voice, both in terms of group outcomes and in terms of group interactions. Amy kept group dynamics at the forefront of her mind and constantly expressed "advisor angst" about the power balance between students and faculty—that is, she struggled with how to step out of her teaching persona and into a different type of relationship with Student Forum members. She admitted that she was used to being in charge, and the students were used to having an adult in charge. She debated whether to let students struggle and sometimes fail and how to coach without taking over. Ultimately, Amy believed that group process was as important as other group outcomes. She therefore consciously worked to share the group leadership with Student Forum members.

Amy pushed the group to think about how to move forward with their ideas by asking questions such as, "What action are you going to take?" rather than offering to set up the process for them. In essence, Amy served the role of a coach rather than taking charge of the meeting. Such scaffolding opportunities provided an avenue for students to model adult roles (Connell, Gambone, & Smith, 1998; Costello, Toles, Spielberger, & Wynn, 2000) as they watched their advisors perform tasks and gradually assume some responsibility for the tasks themselves. Without such continuous attention to creating new roles, it is easy for students and teachers to slip back into traditional roles (Gamson, 1992; Milofsky, 1988; Mitra, 2005). What appeared most important, though, was the angst itself, because it kept the group focused on the power balances within it.

Support of Those in Power. Student Forum also had the strong support of Sean Martin, a leader who could support the group financially, emotionally, and politically. Since Sean controlled the purse strings on the BASRC grant, he was able to provide small increments of funding for conducting the focus groups, for release time for Amy to plan group activities, for students to attend local conferences, and so on. His clout provided resources—especially in terms of information and funding. Amy explained, "If I had to worry about money . . . and the future of the program, it would fall apart. So having someone who's more systemically astute and/or powerful and/or knowledgeable . . . I think that's crucial [to have] someone to do the politics and someone else in the trenches." Sean also served as a group cheerleader, emphasizing the value of the group to Whitman, faculty, and other schools and even reminding Amy and Student Forum youth of the value of their own work. Sean's position of authority on reform in the school therefore provided a source of legitimacy for the group. Sean's knowledge of the system of the school and the district allowed the group to strategically plan its activities to ensure the best possible reception of its work. His knowledge of the full scope of reform activities in the school also provided him with the ability to identify important events and issues and to encourage Student Forum to participate in them, such as developing the schoolwide writing assessments and participating in the teacher research groups on reading strategies. Rosalinda explained, "He gets us places where we need to go and [where] he thinks that we should be. He makes things happen." Sean went a step further to help ensure the success of student voice activities by coaching the youth on how to interact with adults so that they would be heard, such as during staff development sessions and during meetings with the principal.

Creating Sustainable Structures. Most important, perhaps, the group finally developed a meeting structure that allowed for sustained interaction among group members. By developing a formal course that a small group of students could take during the school day, Student Forum members had the opportunity to remain focused on the work of the group throughout the school year. This gift of time and space proved crucial to staying focused on the difficult tasks at hand and initiating enough activities within a school year that the group could feel a sense of accomplishment.

Taking all of these process issues as a whole, the intentional activities of Student Forum and the behind-the-scenes work of Amy and Sean encouraged Whitman faculty members to increase their support of student voice as they came to value the contributions of the students to the school's learning community. Amy observed that she and her colleagues were beginning to work with students regularly in their classrooms to change their curriculum and to receive feedback on their pedagogical strategies. She explained:

> To know kids outside of the classroom is huge and so unique, and
> . . . most teachers have no avenues for doing that. . . . And seeing
> how aware and how knowledgeable and how acutely . . . they know
> what's up. They echo absolutely everything that myself and other

colleagues have talked about in terms of dismay at . . . staff and resources. So . . . heightening my awareness and . . . an appreciation of the kids too. . . . The sense of apathy can be overwhelming . . . because of the things these kids are up against in terms of the neighborhood they live in and the school that they go to. So just seeing their . . . keen awareness, as well as their excitement and willingness and desire to make things better—It's a good shot in the arm.

Opportunities to learn from Student Forum youth kept Amy and her colleagues motivated as teachers and inspired them to continue to improve.

Chapter 7

ENHANCING POSITIVE YOUTH DEVELOPMENT OUTCOMES

If one spent just a small amount of time with Student Forum, it was clear to see that something special was happening with the members. The impact was particularly noticeable in students who otherwise did not find meaning in their school experiences. It could be seen in the way they set their shoulders back when they spoke with adults, the kindness in their discussions with one another, and their pride in their work. Whitman youth acquired important skills that helped them to prepare themselves for the future and to navigate through current situations in their lives. These important changes happening in these students could not be quantified through grade point averages or attendance rates, yet they struck at the core of what needs these youth viewed as most important to their own lives.

These changes experienced by Whitman youth are best described from a research perspective as examples of "positive youth development." From a social context, youth and adults must be able to experience the basic "building blocks of development," including positive relationships, meaningful participation, expectations, and skill building (Eccles & Gootman, 2002; Perkins, Borden, Keith, Hoppe-Rooney, & Villarruel, 2003). The roots of what is now commonly known as a youth development perspective emphasizes the potential for youth to offer resources, opportunities, and assets to their communities (Cahill, 1997; Connell, Gambone, & Smith, 1998; Pittman & Cahill, 1992; Pittman & Wright, 1991). The intention of emphasizing positive youth development is to focus research, policy, and practice on preparing youth for their futures rather than solely preventing risk behaviors.

The youth development field does not possess a consistent set of assets that youth need to acquire to be prepared for the future and to navigate their current situations. However, descriptions of

Table 2. Student Forum Youth Outcomes	
Confidence and compassion	• Being heard • Identifying themselves as change makers • Assuming leadership roles
Connection and caring	• Building stronger relationship with caring adults • Creating a greater connection to their school
Competence and character	• Critiquing their environment • Developing facilitation and problem-solving skills • Respecting others' opinions • Speaking publicly

youth assets in other research focusing on youth development consist of similar types of capacities, including "autonomy, belonging, and competence" (Schapps, Watson, & Lewis, 1997), "self-worth and competence" (Kernaleguen, 1980), "knowledge, belonging and competence" (Villarruel & Lerner, 1994), and "navigation, connection and productivity" (Connell, Gambone, & Smith, 1998). Table 2 summarizes the ways in which Student Forum youth exhibited increases in youth development indicators.

Of all of the lists of positive youth development outcomes, the one most commonly used in the field is "confidence and compassion; connection and caring; competence and character" (National Research Council, 2002; Roth, Brooks-Gunn, Murray, & Foster, 1998). This chapter will therefore describe the growth in Student Forum youth in these three sets of developmental areas. Specifically, participating in these groups helped: (1) to instill confidence in students that they could make a difference and compassion to do so; (2) to establish meaningful connections with adults and peers that strengthen caring and compassion for others; (3) and to build competence and character through acquiring the skills to work toward these changes.

CONFIDENCE AND COMPASSION

A large part of the development of one's identity happens during the high school years. Confidence in a youth development context indicates the courage to exert influence and power in a given situation. Young people with a strong sense of confidence possess agency, self-worth, and a belief that they can make a difference in the world, whether in their own lives or to broader society (Heath & McLaughlin, 1993). When coupled with compassion, young people apply their stronger sense of self toward helping themselves, their peers, and their communities to improve.

One way in which confidence developed among Student Forum members is that they increasingly felt that they were being heard and respected by teachers and administrators in the school. For many, this opportunity was the first time in their lives that they felt they had a voice. Student Forum member Sala Jones, one of the student leaders of the group, explained, "Me being a student, I can really do something. I'm just not an ordinary guy. I have a voice. . . . My opinion counts, and people need to really respect my opinion, to value it." Students' participation in the focus groups and the subsequent analysis created opportunities to be heard from the beginning, and this continued throughout their opportunities to provide teachers with feedback.

Adults in authority positions indicated that they valued the opinions of the students during the student-centered activities. Student Forum member Joey Sampson explained, "We're not just people anymore. We're not just students. We aren't just names anymore. We're actually important, and teachers have to listen to us now as they didn't before. They do now." Teachers demonstrated an increasing desire to collaborate with students on their reform work and a greater receptiveness of youth opinions in class and in staff meetings. Student Forum activities also helped to reduce tension between teachers and students through increasing informality, trust, and learning about one another as more than their school roles and stereotypes.

Student Forum members also developed confidence and compassion as they began to identify themselves as change makers and fostered in themselves a burning desire to work toward positive changes in their school. Schools tend to reinforce preconceived expectations of youth and sort them into categories (Giroux, 1983). Based on these labels, students develop a sense of self. For example, students slotted as "burnouts" in Eckert's (1989) famous study develop an identity based on marginalization and a lack of confidence. Student Forum instead provided opportunities for youth to develop positive forms of identification that are normally unavailable to youth in a school setting. The group members articulated an ability to define new roles for themselves as they pushed the school to redefine itself. Donald Goodwin commented:

> Before [Student Forum], I was just another face in the crowd of students here at Whitman. . . . It kind of makes me feel more powerful now being in this group. . . . I think a lot of students don't even know that when they first come in [to high school] that they can actually do something . . . that they could actually make a change. And since they don't know that, and something goes bad, and they just say, "I'm just going to drop out of school because I don't like it." We need to let them know that they can make a change if they put their minds to it.

Donald's growing sense of self contributed to developing individuality within the school. What is particular about confidence is how it creates the opportunity for youth to develop new identities and roles in their school. Student Forum member Rosalinda Gutierrez transformed perception of school as an obligation she had to fulfill to an opportunity to become a change maker. Over time, Rosalinda increased her participation in Student Forum, including presenting Student Forum's efforts at local teachers' conferences and working intently to explain student perspectives to teachers during staff development sessions. Others noted Rosalinda's transformation, including Sean Martin, who commented, "I've seen some people step forward and actually be able to have their voices heard. Rosalinda comes to mind." Rosalinda's key role as peacemaker helped to smooth tensions and build collegiality among group members. She explained:

> Now I'm very confident in myself. I know that even if there are people that I don't like working with, I could still work with them. I'm actually good at this type of thing—helping others. I know that I can make changes. Sometimes I used to think that our lives were kind of pointless. And it's like, you can make real changes. Now it's the school, and maybe in my career and my adult life I could actually do something, with a lot of determination and a lot of will.

As their confidence grew, Student Forum members also learned to assume leadership roles, which helped to prepare them for adult responsibilities (Connell, Gambone, & Smith, 1998). Leadership emerged in Student Forum members as they assumed responsibility for their group success. Group members improved their articulation of the group's vision and helped facilitate group meetings. Amy Jackson noticed, "Well, [I've seen] just a huge leadership blossoming in a lot of them and an appreciation of each other, [and] working together in different kind of groups." Others observed a growing intention of youth members to assume responsibility for the group, such as Sean Martin, who described freshmen who "sat in the back for two or three meetings, and basically didn't know why the hell they were there. They have become leaders." Martin found this learning process to be crucial to the increase in positive youth development outcomes of the young people in Student Forum.

The youth who participated most in each of the groups displayed the greatest growth in leadership, including guiding the vision and day-to-day tasks of the groups. Twelfth-grade student Sala Jones credited Student Forum with teaching him leadership skills. He commented:

> When a person in school asks me a question, no one knows the amount of joy that I get from being able to give him a straight answer to the problem. When I can talk to someone in a younger grade, and really educate them on what's happening in the school and what you need to do on life, there's no better gratification than to just feel confident that you helped somebody. Student Forum has helped me do that.

These student leaders learned how to encourage the work of others to ensure that the group completed its tasks, and they helped to maintain the vision of the group by reminding their fellow members of the group's purpose and by keeping spirits high. They noticed that their roles in the group helped them to feel more compassionate as they provided assistance to others. They also respected the quiet leadership of other students in the group, according to Sean Martin, who commented,

> The recognition that [veteran] students have of silent people also comes to mind. I see Donald and other students outside of class having conversations with Lata Kumar, for example, who is very quiet. There is a real sense of respect. I'll see them walk up and put

their arms around her and talk with her outside of our meetings. That's real productive.

Thus leadership assumed different forms in the group depending on the personalities and strengths of the youth.

CONNECTION AND CARING

Since youth tend to spend most of their time with peers and relatively little time in formal or informal socialization or interactions with adults, opportunities to develop meaningful connection with adults has become an increasingly important need for adolescents (Csikszentmihalyi & Larson, 1984). Sala Jones explained the great importance of having adults who care in high school:

> I think that relationships between teacher and student throughout their high-school career are the most important thing. . . . Once you have that relationship, you can go to that teacher and you can say, "That's my friend." And they will listen to your problems, whether it has to deal with school or family or girlfriend or whatever, any problem that you have. You can go to them and talk to them. And they'll give you feedback, and they'll be there for you. Just to have people there for you to support you, you will be successful in anything you do.

And indeed, research has demonstrated that building positive relationships with adults is a key component of healthy adolescent development (Kushman, 1997; Moore, 1997). When students believe that they are valued for their perspectives and respected, they begin to develop a sense of ownership and attachment to the organization in which they are involved (Atweh & Burton, 1995). Simply put, they felt that they belonged in their school, and they were proud of it. Attachment, in turn, is positively related to academic success and motivation (Goodenow, 1993; Roeser, Midgley, & Urdan, 1996; Ryan & Powelson, 1991).

Student Forum members built strong relationships with caring adults. Amy and Sean's compassion set a tone for both groups of civility and trust that formed the foundation of the group's interactions. Each possessed a "fire in the belly" (McLaughlin, 1993), meaning they were passionate about young people and structured their careers around a social justice perspective that focused on improving outcomes for youth. Rosalinda explained, "I see ourselves as a family, because I mean everybody cares . . . about every single person that's in the group." "She cares about us," another Student Forum member said of Amy Jackson, "and she cares about the school too. She helps all kinds of students."

Both translated this commitment to a personal level by offering students assistance when they needed help and by sharing their own triumphs and fears with their students. Rosalinda Gutierrez consistently spoke of relying on Amy as a resource. Reflecting on what has helped her grow into an adult during her years at Whitman, she said, "You get information, you get knowledge, and you get to be involved with adults from other careers that you might be interested in. They actually treat you as someone." Beyond support and information, positive interactions with adults also helped to reinforce and strengthen Rosalinda's growing agency.

Most students involved sought advice and information from Amy and Sean on course selection, plans for the future, and dealing with situations at home. For example, Joey Sampson told his mother that he was struggling in trigonometry, and his mother suggested that he drop the class even though he needed it to graduate. Joey and Amy discussed his concern and worked out a way for him to explain to his mother the importance of succeeding in high school and going on to college.

When speaking of building connections, Student Forum members emphasized improved relations with teachers throughout the school. As the group evolved to the goal of building teacher-student partnerships, Student Forum members noticed a greater give and take between teachers and students so that they mutually understood each other and could take action to change the school. Joey Sampson explained, "I think the teachers look at us differently now. Like I kind of like get a little bit more respect, or I know a lot more of them now that I'm involved with this stuff. Because they're like, 'Oh, you're in Student Forum.' Because you're not just another punk kid anymore. You're actually trying to do something."

Students began to understand the perspective of teachers more, and the teachers began to understand the experiences of students. Student Organizer Lana Marcos commented that teachers "recognize you, and they see that you're doing something. It makes you feel like better because they're supporting us and our ideas. So it's not just kind of like, 'Oh, they don't care.' We actually find out they do care. And that means a lot. . . . They opened up a lot by telling us what they go through. . . . That's helped us learn." Student Forum members often spoke of feeling more comfortable speaking to teachers in the hallway and approaching them if they had a concern in class.

The group activity that was particularly instrumental in building connections with teachers was the student-led tours of the local neighborhood. Through interactions of small groups of students and teachers, the tours provided the most meaningful opportunity for teachers and students to learn about each other. Students felt that they truly did come to know their teachers better, and teachers expressed similar sentiments.

Students also developed a stronger connection to the school itself. This connection is critical to adolescent outcomes as seen in the literature on the links between school connection and academic success. Attachment to school is correlated with greater academic success, regardless of students' at-risk status (Damico & Roth, 1991; Fine, 1993; Johnson, 1991). While the design of this study cannot analyze the correlation between academic success and participation in Student Forum, the experiences of group members suggest that they have indeed become more attached to the school. Rosalinda Gutierrez from Student Forum realized the value of affiliation with school and hoped that a Student Forum could be started in other schools in the district as well to help to increase attachment to the school at an earlier age. She commented: "The earlier you get involved, the more students are likely to be interested and more into school in general. Because that is true . . . the earlier you start, the more [you become] involved in other groups, and the better you do in the school."

One way to observe growing attachment was to note the increase in the sense of pride and sense of caring with which Student Forum students began to speak about their school. Jill Bersola, for example, had been afraid to attend Whitman due to its negative and dangerous reputation. She commented, "When I first came to Whitman, I was like, "Oh no, I have to go to a ghetto school." [But] I have learned to love this school . . . Now, I care more about Whitman." Jill mentioned feeling the urge to defend and protect her school rather than to be ashamed of it, which was a sentiment shared by many Student Forum participants.

Some members not only increased their involvement through participation in Student Forum but also became inspired to join other activities. Joey Sampson joined the baseball team and became director of the school play after first becoming involved in Student Forum. He commented:

> Before I was involved in this I didn't want anything to do [with] school. I came to school, did my work, and went home and didn't have anything to do with it. I think I cut most of my math class, so I wasn't even at school when I was supposed to be. I started getting involved in my sophomore year when Ms. Jackson chose me to be in Student Forum. . . . So I came, and it was fun, and I worked with people. I just started wanting to be around school more, started wanting to be involved in more activities and stuff. . . . I noticed that I've got a lot more pride in the school too.

For Joey, Student Forum provided a hook into the school's culture and guided him to other opportunities for interaction.

COMPETENCE AND CHARACTER

By assuming responsibilities in Student Forum and enacting decisions that have consequences for themselves and others, the participating students developed a broad set of competences that helped to build their character and to prepare for adulthood. Youth need to develop new skills and abilities, to actively solve problems, and to be appreciated for their talents (Goodwillie, 1993; Takanishi, 1993; Villarruel & Lerner, 1994). Student Forum members gained, according to Amy Jackson,

> a critical edge and looking at things from a different angle . . . and getting a sense of social justice that I think some of them had definitely already had the seeds of. But giving it a forum for it to develop and for them to practice using that voice and those skills and that lens through which to look at their surroundings.

The group's Ghetto Forums were particularly successful at achieving this focus.

Perhaps one of the most important competencies developed by Student Forum youth was the ability to recognize the problems in their environment and want to change them. Sala Jones asserted,

"If I was a student that was not exposed to this type of thing the knowledge of what goes on within the school may be little depressing. But at least I know it." Sala explained that as a freshman he was not aware of injustices within his school. As a senior, he reflected, "[N]ow I understand. But with it comes a lot of sadness. . . . This is the best way though—I mean, knowing." Students became aware of inequities in their school and learned to question standard practices that were not in the best interest of students.

Student Forum members demonstrated their growth in character building and spoke of the injustices they were beginning to notice in their classrooms during the monthly Student Forum meetings. For example, Joey Sampson talked about hearing students make homophobic remarks in his English class and trying to "set them straight" by explaining why "discrimination against any group was a terrible thing." Despite these advances, the adult advisors of Student Forum hoped to see even further growth in critical thinking. Sean Martin noted that although Joey was growing more aware of injustice in some contexts, he still had much more to learn. He explained, "Joey sits in an English class where what goes on is just bogus. It's a lousy form of education, and he's accepting it. That concerns me. [We] want to have all these kids go into classrooms and be advocates for a strong education. [We want students to] really critique their education. And we have quite a ways to go with that." Sean's disappointment in Joey's lack of outrage demonstrated his hope of increasing the ability of critical thinking skills in all the members of Student Forum. He and Amy encouraged students to become aware of problems and to go beyond identification of concerns to think about how action could be taken to address them.

To be able to discuss their concerns with adults, Student Forum members also had to learn how to speak publicly. Student Forum youth enthusiastically described their growth in this skill. Many of them had been afraid of public speaking, but participating in group activities helped them overcome their fears. Through the practice of making many presentations in Student Forum, students became comfortable sharing their views publicly and did not consider such speaking a difficult task. Rosalinda explained, "I used to be really, really shy, I mean, just shy standing up there. I turned red. I started trembling. It was just bad. And now it's no big deal." Over time Rosalinda began to assume responsibility for large portions of the group's many presentations to adults in the school and in the region.

Even those comfortable with public speaking had some reservations speaking to adults. Joey Sampson, not a shy person in the least, also admitted having initial reservations speaking to adults: "I feel more comfortable speaking in front of large groups of adults. I've always been like a talkative person, but I was uncomfortable speaking in front of large groups of adults, especially educators. But now I don't care."

Student Forum also needed to learn facilitation skills, which helped them to tackle the problems that they identified. Sala Jones asserted, "I've learned a lot about how to run things. Like how to organize things and how to make sure everything's done and tied up all these loose ends that always pop up with something. There's always something else that needs to be done." These facilitation and problem-solving skills that have been identified in previous research are important capacities that youth need to develop (Eckert, 1989; Knight, 1982).

Young people additionally need to learn how to discuss emotional issues in a manner that can lead to constructive solutions. The students most involved in the groups tended to develop an understanding of how to move beyond an awareness of issues to act on their concerns. Student Organizer Lana Marcos explained that she had observed a lot of complaining about problems in her school. Instead she wishes that students would "[s]top and realize that you have power." Lana hoped to help students to move beyond identifying problems to actually taking action to solve them. She continued, "If you really have a passion to have things change . . . come together and do something." Part of this skill set is learning how to address authority and to understand what processes are most likely to achieve positive gains (Goodwillie, 1993; Pittman, Irby, & Ferber, 2000; Takanishi, 1993).

As Student Forum members tackled challenging problems, they especially valued the opportunities to learn about and develop respect for the opinions of others. Through participation in Student Forum activities, they learned to overcome personal biases to become better colleagues. Jaycee Garcia learned not to make assumptions about others. Jaycee explained, "I used to misjudge people. . . . I don't see other people the same way I used to. . . . Because when I got in the group there was a lot of people I didn't

know . . . and I [would think] 'I don't like this girl because she's
stuck up or whatever'. Once you meet the person, it's totally different. . . . I think that made me think about that everybody should be
treated equal." Rosalinda added that Student Forum helped her to
learn how to be "flexible and mature and how to take criticism.
You'll start to view things in a different light too because one
person may not think that's right, so you're going to have to do it
another way. Nobody says, 'Oh, your idea is wrong.' We all listen
to each other." As a result of behaviors such as not prejudging
others, listening more, and controlling one's temper, meetings
became times to exchange opinions, to develop meaningful relationships with peers, and to learn from one another.

Sala Jones, who possessed strong leadership skills before participating in Student Forum, learned to listen more and speak less.
He commented, "I learned how to bite my tongue. I learned how
to hear out people a little bit more. I learned how to facilitate. I
mean, these things I take for granted now, that I learned how to
do. And I get so accustomed to doing it, but it's taught me proba-
bly a whole lot more than I recognize right now."

Joey Sampson instead needed to learn how to control his
anger. Participating in Student Forum taught him how to control
his emotions. He reflected, "I used to get in arguments with a lot
of people before, because I have a hard time controlling my anger.
I'll start an argument sometimes just to get in a verbal fight with
somebody. . . . Now I tend to talk things out more before I get
mad at somebody. . . . It's just a lot easier for me to have an actual
conversation now than an argument." Joey stopped trying to insti-
gate fights and instead sought dialogue among Student Forum
members and the broader school

THE IMPORTANCE OF SCHOOL-BASED YOUTH ADULT PARTNERSHIPS

Efforts to increase student voice can create meaningful experiences
that help to meet the developmental needs of youth, particularly
for those students who otherwise did not find meaning in their
school experiences. The experiences of young people in Student
Forum suggest that student voice efforts can foster conditions that
help youth to achieve the fundamental building blocks of development. Participating in these groups helped Whitman students to

believe that they could transform themselves and the institutions that affect them, to establish greater connections with their peers and with adults, and to acquire the skills and competencies to work toward the needed changes in their schools. Particularly significant was the fact that the youth who otherwise did not find meaning in their school careers experienced fundamental growth through participating in Student Forum.

While these data point toward the potential of student voice efforts, the consistent findings of confidence and compassion, connection and caring, and competence and character in these students also help to validate the existence of a core set of youth developmental needs. In fact, research in developmental psychology finds these six traits to be necessary factors for adolescents to remain motivated in school and to achieve academic success (Eccles, Midgley, Wigfield, Buchanan, et al., 1993; Goodenow, 1993; Roeser, Midgley, & Urdan, 1996; Stinson, 1993). An interesting facet of the growth in Student Forum youth was that student voice opportunities addressed a wide variety of student needs rather than a one-size-fits-all approach. Students with low self-concepts, like Rosalinda and Lata, had opportunities to build confidence; others, lacking a meaningful connection to school, such as Jill and Bailey, had an opportunity to build stronger ties; and students in need of developing specific skills such as public speaking and getting along with others had opportunities to do so, including Joey and Sala. Furthermore, changes were greater for the youth with a stronger involvement in their respective group. The most involved students demonstrated the greatest shifts of the youth members. The experiences further suggest that the greater the youth leadership in student voice activities, the greater the benefit for youth. Other research has demonstrated the connection between greater youth leadership and improved student outcomes as well (deCharms, 2001; Earl & Lee, 1999; Johnson, 1991; Lee & Zimmerman, 2001).

Additionally, the experiences of Whitman youth fit with the broader literature on youth-adult partnerships that indicates that youth engagement in meaningful tasks is most fruitful when the benefits extend beyond the individual and link him/her to the surrounding community (Pancer, Rose-Krasnor, & Loisell, 2002). Opportunities to address community issues and improve the quality of life for a young person's broader community, whether it be her school or her neighborhood, may enhance her civic competence and social networks while also fostering feelings of social responsibility (Checkoway, et al., 2003). Thus, the greater impact these young people can make in their schools, the greater gains for their own growth and development.

Chapter 8

STUDENT VOICE AS AN AVENUE FOR CHANGE

The successful efforts of Student Forum suggest that student voice can serve as a catalyst for broadening leadership in schools and progress toward substantive change. The greater the problems in a school, the greater the need for students to "make it real" by naming the problems and helping to address them. The notion of "distributed leadership" typically has been defined in educational leadership circles as sharing decision making with teachers or the development of coprincipals (Copeland, 2003; Elmore, 2000; Lashway, 2003). Research on student voice has indicated that when students take a greater role in leadership practices in schools, it can lead to improvements in instruction, curriculum, testing policy, assessment systems, and teacher-student relationships (Colatos & Morrell, 2003; Cook-Sather, 2002; Fielding, 2001; Soohoo, 1993). The findings of this study support this previous research. In particular, this book has demonstrated the importance of attending to group process in student voice initiatives. The study also has highlighted the ways that Student Forum worked toward improving schoolwide outcomes by gaining a voice in the school's professional learning community. The findings from this study also provide particularly strong evidence for ways in which student voice initiatives can contribute to positive youth development outcomes for the young people involved.

Attending to Group Process Was Essential to Positive Outcomes for Whitman's Youth-Adult Partnership. Moving student voice efforts to the point that they are able to effect change in schools is undoubtedly a challenge because of the institutional constraints on the level of authority that they can assume in a school. Student Forum's success in overcoming the inertia of traditional student roles in large part can be attributed to several group strategies. Before the group was able to engage the meat of school change, Student Forum first needed to establish common norms and vision that would establish a sharing of power and responsibility among young people and adults in the partnership. The group also needed a strong adult advocate, Amy Jackson, who was able to buffer the group from criticism and to build bridges with the faculty and other school groups that could strengthen the legitimacy and reach of Student Forum's efforts. Student Forum also received the support of a savvy person in the school, Sean Martin, who was able to provide the group with financial resources, emotional support, and connections to key opportunities. Last, the group needed to create sustainable structures that would allow the group to increase their collaboration time and ability to focus sufficient ongoing time toward their project goals.

Improving Schoolwide Outcomes. A year and a half of capacity building was needed at Whitman to move from reflection on focus group data to a series of actions intended to improve teacher-student communication. Once this capacity was achieved, the group quickly accomplished many schoolwide outcomes. By developing "teacher-focused" and "student-focused" activities, Student Forum helped to strengthen the school's professional learning community so that it could improve its efforts to strengthen the school's teaching and learning outcomes. Student Forum members provided pedagogical feedback to faculty, including information on how students would receive new instructional strategies, on how to translate teacher strategies into language that students would understand, and on ways to teach young people about the reforms happening in their school so that they could understand and share in the ownership of the change process. Student Forum also provided needed inspiration and motivation to school faculty to persist their hard road toward school improvement. Having young people participate in professional learning community activities helped the teachers to prioritize their tasks to serve the best interests of students. It also helped to preserve a collegial tone in a usually very contentious school climate. Last, Student Forum increased the willingness to further the school's youth-adult partnership. Collaboration bred the desire for future partnership as teachers came to see the benefits and rewards of including student voices in the school's professional learning community activities.

Increasing Positive Youth Development Outcomes. The experiences of Student Forum demonstrate that student voice can address youth development concerns, student alienation, and high school intransigence. Student Forum youth increased their ownership in the school, built a source of intrinsic motivation, acquired the skills and competence to work toward these changes, and established meaningful relationships with adults and the peers that created greater connections to each other. In a time when practitioners face growing pressure to emphasize standardized testing, the powerful youth development outcomes experienced by the young people in Student Forum highlight the importance of a broader definition of the important skills and assets that youth need to learn to prepare themselves for the future and to navigate through current situations in their lives.

In this research, students identified three areas of growth in particular. They spoke of an increase in "confidence and compassion," or a belief that they can make changes in their environment and that their voices deserve to be heard and will be. They also spoke of an increased sense of "connection and caring" to the school, to school personnel, and to their peers; for some this was the first time that they felt that they "belonged" in their school. The young people also spoke of learning "competence and character" that they had never had the opportunity to learn before, including how to critique their communities to identify problems and address them, how to facilitate meetings and work with others, how to respect others' opinions and learn to get along with others who are different from them, and how to speak publicly in an articulate manner that would be well received by adults. Young people in this research consistently expressed enthusiasm, and even gratefulness, for the opportunities that they had to develop these qualities of confidence and compassion; connection and caring; and competence and character.

THE FUTURE OF STUDENT VOICE

This book has demonstrated the potential value of student voice initiatives for schools and for the young people involved in these efforts. Through describing the evolving nature of Student Forum at Whitman, it has emphasized the importance of the process by which student voice initiatives are developed and the benefits of such school-based youth-adult partnerships for the school and youth as well. To increase opportunities for students and to help them grow, young people must assume some leadership in the student voice initiative. The more students can assume agency in the initiatives, the more opportunities they have to learn and to grow. And the greater the development of youth leadership, the greater the possibility for collaboration and distributed leadership that can lead to changes in their schools and in broader society.

Unfortunately, most schools are not structured in ways that encourage student voice; instead they often conflict with adolescent needs (Costello et al., 2000). Structural issues such as large school and class size increase student alienation. Segregation by age and ability prevents students from learning from more experienced peers. A view of students as "clients" increases the sense of distance between teachers and students. Pressure from districts and states to prove school successes forces a compulsion to sweep controversies under the rug and breeds an unwillingness to tolerate and support the differences of opinion that student voice requires.

The intransigence of high schools and the subsequent epidemic of student alienation might in large part be caused by the lack of opportunities to situate students as essential actors in school decision making. Researchers can help schools begin to construct new student roles by continuing to share the experiences of schools that have begun to incorporate student voice into school reform and classroom practice. The work of Student Forum suggests strategies that can help to create a subtle shift in school culture. By developing activities that were both "teacher-focused" and "student focused," Student Forum developed a strategy that helped to build trust and understanding rather than to increase divisiveness between teachers and students. To accomplish the smallest of victories required Student Forum to struggle against the inertia of conscious and unconscious beliefs and procedures that tend to suppress the voices of students and their value in contributing to more effective decision making in schools.

As practitioners, researchers, and policymakers continue to ask questions about the process and influence of student voice in school reform, knowledge of the implications of student voice will continue to grow. Through further research, it will be possible to deepen theoretical and empirical understandings regarding the possibility of student voice for altering the dynamics of schools and improving teaching and learning. In the words of an inspiring student leader at Whitman High School, Joey Sampson promised, "Changes are happening. They may be happening slowly, but they are happening. We are hacking away at the machine, and we will be heard."

Appendix

METHODOLOGY

One of the greatest criticisms of qualitative research is that most studies do not make explicit how the researcher proceeded from research questions to final conclusions. The few studies that have carefully explained the process of collecting and analyzing data include research by Annette Lareau (1989b), Jay MacLeod (1987), and Melanie Moore (1997). These researchers detailed each step of their research process, from their initial questions, to reach their conclusions. Especially helpful in these studies was their willingness to share "warts and all" by acknowledging mistakes and concerns about their analysis as well as their successes. In the spirit of such works, I offer this appendix as a candid and thorough record of how I conducted my research at Whitman High School.

FINDING WHITMAN

I was first introduced to Whitman High School at the BASRC annual conference in May 1999. As described in chapter 2, it was the last afternoon of the meeting, and people were tired. I was one of the conference participants heading toward a session when I noticed high school students in the hallway outside of one room working their hardest to entice people to attend their presentation. I later learned that these three young men—Joey, Sala, and Donald—were three of the most active and articulate members of the Student Forum group. Sitting in that conference room, it was clear that the story of this inspired group needed to be shared, and I wanted to be the one to do so.

Gaining access to work with Whitman was fairly easy. I was a member of the research team at Stanford University's Center for the Context of Teaching, which was conducting an evaluation of BASRC. As part of our evaluation, we closely followed ten BASRC schools over five years. My purpose at the conference was to collect data on some other schools in the initiative. As fate would have it, Whitman was added as a case study school at about the same time as the group's Collaborative Assembly presentation. I eagerly assumed responsibility for the case.

The scope of the BASRC evaluation extended as far an examination of student voice. To fulfill my responsibilities for the BASRC evaluation, my job was to gain a clear understanding of all of the reform work happening at Whitman. I conducted interviews with teachers, students, and administrators twice a year and observed important meetings and school events over the past two years.

During my first interview with Sean Martin, I made clear my interests in wanting to research the involvement of students at Whitman as a separate study. Sean warmly accepted the idea and asked me to write a letter describing my study, which he would share with the principal to inform him of my work. Fitting with his inclusive nature, Sean also shared the letter with all of the students participating in the focus groups. He explained that since we were all partners, it was important that everyone had a copy of the letter explaining my work.

When I attended Student Forum meetings, I tried to sit quietly in the back of the room, but undoubtedly my typing on my laptop raised questions. During a time for questions in the first organizational meeting of the year, described in chapter 3, a student turned to me and said, "Who's she?" I took the opportunity to describe my role as a "documenter" of what happens at these meetings as a part of the BASRC evaluation. I explained that this would help other schools to learn about Whitman's work on changing their school. I also explained that I was present because I was writing a book on student voice at Whitman.

DATA COLLECTION

I systematically sought multiple perspectives in my research. I relied on several sources during my data collection in this study—observations, interviews, and documents. The bulk of my fieldwork took place during the 1999–2000 school year. I spent most of my research time observing meetings, conducting iterative interviews with many individuals, and "hanging out" when possible to gain a deeper understanding of the work of the groups. At the end of the 2000–2001 school year, Student Forum developed a Student Forum Organizer structure. I continued data collection of meetings and interviews throughout the fall and to a limited extent throughout the year.

Observations. To gain a full picture of the groups that I studied, I observed as many meetings as possible to watch for changes over time. I tried to understand what was unspoken and to interpret what was. My main goal during my observations of meetings and informal interactions was to examine the internal process of Student Forum. Through observations I had the opportunity to observe firsthand Student Forum's group dynamics as a way to examine such issues as how decisions were made, who assumed what roles, and what norms they shared.

My purpose at Whitman was not as a participant observer but rather as an outside observer. When observing meetings, I took a seat in the back of the room. I never participated unless directly asked a question. My intention during observations was to capture the words of individuals directly with little summarizing or interpretation. When observing meetings larger than three people, I transcribed them word for word when possible on my laptop. This allowed me to capture events as they were happening in the most accurate way possible. Undoubtedly, I missed some nonverbal communication. However, I did read through these notes nightly to cleanse and prepare them and added nonverbal interactions at this time.

When I did have opinions to share about what I was seeing, I noted in brackets how the members of the group interacted, what roles were assumed by whom, how decisions were made, what norms and shared concepts developed and from where, and how they talked about the purpose of the group and its future. During interactions with outsiders, I looked for similar issues, but I also focused on how the group members portrayed themselves and how the outside individuals perceived Student Forum. For example, I looked at how legitimate the work seemed to the outsiders and how confident the group seemed in what they intended, whether the vision of the group shifted when questions were asked, and whose voices within the group seemed to be most valued as representing the group and valued by outsiders as in charge. During my analyses I often later found that these observations were not as relevant to the big picture of the events as I thought at the time, perhaps because as my research evolved I looked for different sorts of things from the data. Having a record that separated these insights from my transcription allowed me to revisit these observations on a regular basis to look for fresh ideas.

As a courtesy and a way to give back to the group, I would send transcripts of meetings, with all commentary or analysis removed, to both Sean and Amy so that they could use these to reflect on what had happened and how to move forward in the work. They told me that they found these transcripts helpful for keeping a history of the group and referring back to what happened as they planned for the next meeting. This resource was easy for me to produce, and I did not feel that it greatly influenced their decision making.

My goal was to be present at nearly all of the formal meetings throughout the year and also observe informal conversations between group members and with adults. Between my research and my evaluation responsibilities, I was present at the school on average two days a week throughout the 1999–2000 school year. In the fall of 2000, I was present about two to three times a month.

Student Forum did not have a regular schedule of meetings but they usually met once or twice a month as a large group. For each large group meeting there was at least one smaller planning meeting. I estimate that I was able to attend approximately 90 percent of the Student Forum large group meetings. I was unable to attend meetings during periods of time during the year when I experienced illness (mid-December until mid-January), family emergencies (three weeks in March), and professional responsibilities (two weeks in April). When I missed a critical event, I would ask as many students and adults as I could find to tell me what happened and what they felt about what happened.

In addition to having other responsibilities that kept me away from Whitman, occasionally meetings would occur, either planned or impromptu, that I did not know about. One of the trade-offs of being an outside observer was that the groups did not always keep me informed of changes in their schedules. It was necessary to drop by the school when things seemed not to be happening to find out what was truly going on, which was sometimes difficult since I lived 45 minutes away. Once the Student Organizers started meeting every day, I also missed much more of the stronger decision making since I could not be at the school all of the time. Nevertheless, after attending meetings for about a year, Amy and Sean started to contact me when important events were happening, both because they knew that I would be interested and because I was able to provide them with a transcript of the meeting.

Capturing the significant moments in Student Forum's evolution also proved difficult because student voice at Whitman did not have a formal "place." Unlike much school research, I did not have a particular classroom to visit or an office to go to where I could observe the topic of my study on a regular basis. When I would drop by, the question of where to go to observe informal interactions of the group proved difficult. Outside of formal meetings, important conversations happened in the hallways during passing periods, or Amy or Sean would spontaneously pull students out of class to touch base. When I did miss meetings or unscheduled key events that I did not know to attend, I attempted to interview both adults and youth immediately upon my return to capture multiple perspectives of the events that occurred.

Interviews. To improve the validity of my research, I sought as many different perspectives as possible on student involvement, including students, teachers, administrators, and outside consultants. I also interviewed all students who participated in the Student Forum regularly and a few students who came intermittently. I also interviewed Sean and Amy several times. For all of the main actors in the case, I used an iterative process of interviewing, talking to them twice—once toward the beginning of the school year, and once at the end. Since Student Forum continued into the following year, I interviewed these students and advisors for a third time in the fall. In addition to these interviews, throughout my data collection, I interviewed the principal, other teachers in the school, and the school's outside consultant that provides support on school reform.

The iterative interview process and the variety of individuals interviewed contribute to the reliability of my data. I recorded all interviews on audiocassette to preserve the words of the interviewees. When I received them from the transcriber, I would "cleanse" them for accuracy by listening to the tape and correcting any errors on the document. When I engaged in important informal conversations with adults or students, I would either write them up by memory when I returned home or talk into a tape recorder as I drove home. I did stick to the researcher's creed of "never sleeping on my field notes." I always either dictated or typed them up that same day, so they maintain a high level of accuracy of what was said.

My interviews were semistructured. When conducting interviews, my intent was not to follow a predetermined protocol. I would prepare approximately eight main issues that I wanted to cover with the interviewee. I tended to start with an open question that would allow the interviewee to tell his story in the way in which he was most comfortable. In my first round of interviews, I gathered baseline data on the nature of collaboration at the schools and the general climate, with a particular focus on types of activities the group wanted to do and the type of group culture that was developing. As the year progressed, I expanded my questioning to include the changes in individuals and the group, including how the group worked together and the changes that it wanted to accomplish. I also asked adults about the types of support that they provided to assist students, and I asked students about the supports they needed from adults.

In initial interviews I began with, "Tell me how you first got involved in the group." In my last round of interviews I began with, "So what are the main things the group is working on right now?" Other important questions included:

Why did you get involved?
• Why have you stayed involved? What makes it meaningful to you?
• Are you involved in any other organizations in the school?

What types of students does the group involve?
• Why weren't they connected to the school before?
• What is special about this group?

Is the group what you expected it would be?
• What are the greatest accomplishments of the group so far?
• Do you think it's made any changes in the school?
• What do you like best about it? What could be improved?
• Do you feel that you have changed because of being involved in the group?

Describe the roles of students and adults in Student Forum
• Who plays different roles? What role do you play?
• What would happen to the group if Amy and Sean were not here next year?

- How is a decision made in the group?
- Any examples where there was a disagreement in the group? Tell me about it; how was it resolved?

Overall what would you say the role of students should be in reforming Whitman?
- What would you tell other schools who wanted to increase student voice?
- What should I write in my book?
- Are there places students don't belong?

After touching on the key issues from my research questions that I wanted to cover in that interview, I would normally end with a "pie-in the-sky" question (such as, "If you could change anything about your school, what would it be?"). Often I would remind them that I was writing a book and ask, "What do you want others to most know about the work you're doing here at Whitman in this group? What would you tell other schools who wanted to start a similar program?"

I conducted most interviews in the school's library. It was large enough that I could usually find a table in the back that was fairly quiet. Few students wandered through there so my interviewees were rarely distracted, although there were times, when classes came to the library to work, that the noise became loud on my recorder. I often would also use Amy Jackson's room for Student Forum group interviews after I noticed that students did not seem to notice when she was in or out of the room. The library closed during lunchtime, so Amy's room offered one of the few quiet places where I knew I could go to conduct interviews or to fill in my field notes. Students seemed to feel comfortable saying whatever they chose in front of her. I would, however, try to reserve asking questions directly about the advisors until she stepped out of the room to help to ensure that students would not feel inhibited to say how they felt.

I do not believe that any of the interviewees intentionally misled me in any manner. Nonetheless, each brought a unique perspective and broader set of contexts that colored their interpretation of events. I continued to interview the actors in this study on a regular basis until I felt I was "saturated" with the data, which for me meant when I felt that I could predict much of what an interviewee would say. I feel that I reached the saturation point with all

of the main characters in the study, which I would classify as all
adults and students in the charts of group members provided in the
case chapters. Saturation meant that I had developed a sufficient
understanding of their broader contexts to situate their responses
within their frame of reference in the group.

Document Analysis. During these two years I also collected
written documentation available from the groups, including internal documents and those meant for an external audience. The documents demonstrated what was valued by the school community
and beyond the walls of the school, including to what extent the
student contribution is viewed as a priority. Since student voice
began at Whitman the spring prior to my research, documents
provide key information about what happened during this time.
They also were helpful after I arrived as a way of viewing how the
groups formally expressed their vision and plans to the broader
school community.

Documents also helped to verify the demographic information of Whitman. The demographic facts presented especially at
the beginning of chapter 3 were confirmed by the school's data
technician. They were also compared to the information provided
in Whitman's "Review of Progress" document prepared for
BASRC in January 2000, which was an annual report articulating
Whitman's reform process as a form of accountability for receiving
ongoing grant funding.

Considering the Data Collection Overall. Table 3 provides a sum-
mary of the interviews, observations, and documents collected over
the course of this research. The table includes data not only about
the two cases but also on the data from other staff members and
events at Whitman that were relevant to student involvement,
including many essential interviews with Sean Martin. Since he
provided reflections on all of the groups plus other events at the
school, I listed his data separately. I view him as my most valuable
adult informant. He had a keen understanding of how reform
works and a careful finger on the pulse of the school. He also
probably thought more about how to move forward the work on
student voice than any other individual in the school, student or
adult.

As the table indicates, data were not collected at a uniform
rate; the rate fluctuated depending on the amount of activity in the
group. My observations increased as the group continued to build

Table 3. Data Collection over Time

	1998–1999 school year	1999–2000 school year	2000–2001 school year	Total
Meeting observations	1	14	10	25
Student interviews	1	16	5	22
Amy Jackson interviews	1	3	1	5
Sean Martin interviews	1	11	5	17
Documents	10	13	1	24
Interviews with other staff and students	2	27	2	31

momentum. Student Forum Organizers met daily in fall 2000, which allowed for many more observation opportunities than the previous year when the group met only once or twice a month. When observation opportunities were scant, I focused more time on interviews. I relied most on documents before I began my data collection. Once I began going to Whitman regularly, my own observations and interviews proved more useful.

RESEARCHER ROLE

As my time with these groups continued, maintaining my status as an outside observer became increasingly more difficult. In April 2000, I encountered my first true breach of neutrality beyond sharing transcript notes. Student Forum members were feeling pressed to complete all of the tasks they needed to do before their April membership drive. One task was to develop a way to express their purpose as a group. During a planning meeting, the students decided that they needed an official name. I mentioned that lots of groups have mission statements and explained what they were. The students asked if I would be willing to explain the notion of a mission statement and why the group might want to have one. I agreed to step out of my researcher role to help with this activity. At the large group meeting the next day, after explaining the concept of a mission statement, the students wrote down what key issue they would want to be sure was included in a mission statement. At the end of the meeting I asked for volunteers to get together before the next meeting to draft the mission statement.

The following week I facilitated three students in compiling the ideas from the student papers in the meeting into one mission statement for the group. Interestingly, three of the quietest girls in the group volunteered to work on this project. Jaycee signed up, along with a shy Punjabi girl named Lata, who had moved to the United States two years before. The third girl was Troy Newman's quiet girlfriend. Their volunteering for the project may have occurred because the task involved writing rather than speaking or facilitating, and writing was one of their strengths. They may also have been more willing because I agreed to facilitate the group, and I had spoken with each of these girls throughout the year as a part of my data collection and attempts to get perspectives from all participants in the group, not just those who chose to speak up at meetings. Regardless, during our work that day, I was careful not to insert my views of what the mission statement should say. I spread out all of the suggestions from the last meeting on the table and worked with the students to place similar suggestions together. I then wrote up all of the main ideas that the group wanted to include in the mission statement. The girls decided what wording they liked best, and we placed it together into one statement. The girls presented their work to the larger group at the next meeting.

After assisting with the mission statement work, I tried to return to the role of researcher as best I could. Other than sharing transcripts, my other interaction with students and adults was informal conversation outside of the meetings. I came to learn more about their lives, and they learned about mine. With Lata, I eventually assumed a mentoring role separate from the group. She was applying to college, but her father did not believe that it was proper for a Punjabi girl to leave the home. Her struggles with her family and her goals to become a physician caused enormous stress for her. I served as a shoulder for her to cry on, sometimes literally. I also offered advice on applying to colleges. I gave feedback on her college essay. And when she received her acceptances, I took her to the local state college options she was obligated to attend so that she could live at home, despite her acceptances to University of California schools farther away. I helped her file her registration forms, learn her way around the campus and visit the bookstore. In the summer, I returned with her to register for classes and to convince the bursar to wait a bit longer for payment of her bill. I still keep in touch with her, primarily through e-mail. She sends me questions about her assignments, and I help her to find resources on the Internet.

My relationships with the other members of the group did not develop to the extent that they did with Lata, although I tried to assume the role of "cheerleader" with most of them, trying to encourage and support what they were doing. With adults and students, I tried not to be placed in the role of critic and tried not to offer advice. Nonetheless, when asked "point blank" my reflections, I did not feel that it was appropriate to refuse to give them. After the second Collaborative Assembly presentation, Amy and Sean asked me to meet and to share with them what I thought were the main pieces of feedback the audience had expressed to the group. I shared what I had heard as the most important points and asked them if they had heard the same things. The discussion was a mutual exchange of ideas, a way of crosschecking our interpretations of the experience.

As I spent more time with the individuals in my study, undoubtedly I became more attached to them, and them to me. I never consciously tried to portray a more positive picture of the experiences of the group—in fact the nature of Sean and Amy in particular was such that they invited critical feedback as much as kudos, if not more so. Nonetheless, if there is a bias in my data, it is respect and admiration for the efforts of adults and students at Whitman High School who engaged in this difficult work.

DATA ANALYSIS

My strategies for data analysis were guided by grounded theory (Glaser & Strauss, 1967; Strauss & Corbin, 1990), which is a qualitative methodology useful for developing theory that is "grounded in data systematically gathered and analyzed" (Strauss & Corbin, 1994, p. 273). Theory in this case is defined as "plausible relations among concepts and sets of concepts" (Strauss & Corbin, 1994, p. 278). Grounded theory was especially useful for describing student voice efforts at Whitman since it focuses on moving beyond description to developing theory by making connections, defining relationships, and looking for patterns of action between concepts derived from the data.

Given the smaller scope of my research and that I conducted the study alone, my reduction and analysis process described below is more concise than Strauss and Corbin's systematic coding steps, which entail multiple coding processes. Nonetheless, I believe it still retains the intentions and spirit of grounded theory. Additionally, many of the procedures of grounded theory are similar to those of other qualitative methods. Therefore, I also drew upon other qualitative data analysis strategies, including those detailed by Matthew Miles and Michael Huberman (1994) and Howard Becker (1998).

Data Reduction. To move from raw data to conclusions, I engaged in a process of data reduction that allowed me to break data down, conceptualize it, and put it back together in new ways. This was no easy task. With more than three years of data collection, the piles of transcripts, field notes, and documents on my desk proved daunting. I began my data reduction by writing out a detailed chronological draft of the Student Forum case.

I reviewed meeting notes and interviews as the first step of analyzing Student Forum's experiences over the school year. I attempted to summarize what I found and cut and pasted important quotes into new files. In doing so, I broke down the data into discrete parts, looking for similarities and differences between events and individual interpretations. Writing a first draft of the case provided a way to identify initial categories that best fit the text (Miles & Huberman, 1994), including process, reasons for joining the group and continuing to participate, individual and group visions of Student Forum, and the actual tasks attempted.

As I incorporated more data into the narrative, I looked for patterns that supported or refuted my interpretation of the data. I relied on several perspectives to characterize each critical incident in the case, and I considered these opinions within the broader context of the interviewees' perspectives and experiences. Thus, I trusted each perspective to the extent that it provided one lens onto a situation. Through viewing many such lenses of interview data, my analysis provides a description of shared interpretations of group events and also incidences when individuals disagreed with the party line.

When I finally finished this task several days and uncountable hours later, the opus was almost 50 single-spaced pages. Certainly it was not something that would be shared widely, but it provided an opportunity to recount the events and to begin to reflect on the data. Following this larger draft, I wrote a memo that summarized the themes, and I described what I felt Student Forum "was a case of" (Ragin, 1992)—that is, the main contributions of the case to theory and to understanding student voice at Whitman. Becker (1998) suggests that a way to move beyond description is to find a way to explain what one has found in the data without using any of the identifying characteristics of the actual case. The intent in the memo was to move beyond the data in a similar fashion—not to summarize the larger chronological writeup, but rather to find multiple instances and events that fit under bigger categories.

I decided upon main bins for coding based on my initial writeup of the Student Forum case. I also considered coding trees from other research projects to provide other ideas for how to sort data. Part of this initial coding was defining the relational nature of these categories by identifying their properties and dimensions (Becker, 1998; Strauss & Corbin, 1990). To do so, I added sub-codes beneath larger bins that appeared too large. My initial main coding bins are listed in Table 4.

After developing the coding tree, I coded all 214 data pieces. To manage my data, I used QSR Nud*ist, a qualitative data analysis program. The program assists with data storage and retrieval such that it allowed me to search for patterns in the material and to locate discrepancies and missing pieces. My coding process included writing the codes on the transcripts, cleansing the documents for errors and formatting them for QSR Nud*ist, importing files into the QSR Nud*ist program, and entering in the codes. I coded the documents in batches, starting with Student Forum members and then moving on to interviews with other Whitman staff and students and observations of other school events.

Developing a Framework. After drafting the cases and writing an analytic memo, I felt that I had the data sorted in two ways—thematically and chronologically. I then conducted data "runs"—meaning I asked questions of the data and used QSR Nud*ist software to search for combinations of codes that helped to organize the data so that I could answer my questions. This helped me to move beyond open coding of sorting themes to begin to develop a framework for analysis.

The purpose of an explanatory framework is to determine the central phenomenon around which to relate other categories

Table 4. Main Codes for Data Analysis

Process: This code helped to separate components for analysis of how the groups work together, including decision making, adult-student power balances, advisor roles, and group norms. I also coded for student experiences, including interaction between youth and distinctions made between veteran and newcomer members.

Outcomes: This chunk of codes provided a place to bookmark important data for analysis of "what difference did student voice make at Whitman?" Codes included student outcomes, adult outcomes, and school-level outcomes. Student outcome codes included attachment to school, increased interaction with adults, self-concept/confidence, and improved interaction with students.

Conceptions: This code was used for indicating people's perceptions of the current work and speculations of the work to come. It allowed me to consider what people consider to be the vision of the work and where it was headed.

Context: This set of codes provided a place to catalog details about the characters and settings in this story, which allowed for richer description of the story in my writing.

Activities and action: This set of codes allowed me to pull out subplots and ongoing strands of group activity.

Organizational concerns: This set of codes was useful for examining the connection between Student Forum and the broader school. Subcodes included issues such as legitimacy, sustainability, and resources.

Bookmarks: These codes served as punctuation marks for the most salient quotations and issues throughout my data.

(Miles & Huberman, 1994, Strauss & Corbin, 1990). Becker (1998) describes this procedure as stripping away what is accidentally or coincidentally present to identify the core phenomenon of the study by examining what must be present for the phenomenon to exist. The purpose is to isolate the generic features that a series have in common.

Rather than proceeding linearly from coding to framework revision, I considered each in tandem. Each round of coding raised more questions and caused a further review of my framework, which cased further categorization of my data. After much reflection and many conversations with Milbrey McLaughlin, I decided that a youth development perspective seemed to be the missing piece in my analysis of youth experience with student voice. Using the QSR Nud*ist program, I was able to sort and gather all of these pieces of information throughout the data. I used this compilation to search for repeating themes in the responses and observations and bean sorting the data into categories.

Overall, the data can support broader patterns through which to understand the youth experiences. Certain generalizations could be made because they were stark—such as the smaller, more intensively involved members (i.e., the Student Organizers) demonstrated more growth and in a wider variety of categories than less involved students. And it also was possible to identify categories in which one group had dramatically stronger data than the other.

I would like to have analyzed the data for categories and then used these bins to construct a survey or interview protocol and to administer to all of the members of each group. But my analysis took longer than expected, and most have since moved on to college, the armed services, or jobs and thus would be difficult or impossible to find.

Validity Checks. To help ensure validity of my analysis, and particularly in the final year, I shared my findings with a variety of individuals. In addition to sharing my work with colleagues at Stanford and other universities, I informally shared my findings with Whitman adults and youth. Sean and Amy particularly gave feedback on my findings.

My initial intention was to formally share my analysis with all of the adults and youth at Whitman who worked on student voice. Yet, my few attempts to do so did not prove as helpful as I had expected. When presenting findings, the students in particular, but also the adults, would nod their heads and express interest in what I had concluded. They did not object to my findings and yet did not engage in them in a detailed manner. It became clear to me that an academic analysis of their work was my "enterprise," not theirs. And they seemed to be quite content with that. I was less satisfied and yet accepted this decision as their choice. Sean Martin was the one exception, and several times he and I discussed the details of my findings, the causes of them, and the consequences of the work of the two groups.

I also validated my data by comparing it to findings from survey research that we were conducting at Whitman and other reforming schools to evaluate the BASRC (Center for Research on the Context of Teaching, 2002). In fact, teacher survey data demonstrated a growth in student voice at Whitman. Chapter 6 of this book briefly discusses these data. A survey was administered to all teachers at Whitman in February 2001. One of the sections on the survey focused on how reform has impacted the school, asking: "Indicate how, if at all, your school has changed in the last five years." The teachers responded to approximately 15 questions that included a variety of issues such as professional development, inquiry, changes in decision making, and changes in classroom practice. They indicated their answers using a five-point Likert scale that offered the following options: substantial decrease, some decrease, no change, some increase, substantial increase. When responding to the prompt "student voice in school decisions," the full results were "substantial decrease-0%, some decrease-2%, no change-12%, some increase-62%, substantial increase-23%."

WORKS CITED

Achinstein, B. (2002). *Community, diversity, and conflict among schoolteachers: The ties that bind.* New York: Teachers College.

Atweh, B., & Burton, L. (1995). Students as researchers: Rationale and critique. *British Educational Research Journal, 21*(5), 561–575.

Bauch, P. A., & Goldring, E. B. (1998). Parent-teacher participation in the context of school governance. *Peabody Journal of Education, 73*(1), 15–35.

Becker, H. S. (1998). *Tricks of the trade: How to think about research while you're doing it.* Chicago: University of Chicago Press.

Binder, A. (2002). *Contentious curricula: Afrocentrism and creationism in American public schools.* Princeton: Princeton University Press.

Blase, J. (1991). Everyday political perspectives of teachers toward students. *The politics of life in schools: Power, conflict, and cooperation.* Newbury Park: Sage.

Bridgeland, J. M., Dilulio, Jr., J. J., and Morison, K. B. (2006). *The silent epidemic: Perspectives of high school dropouts.* Civic Enterprises/Peter D. Hart Research Associates.

Brown, J. S., & Duguid, P. (2000). *Social life of information.* Boston: Harvard Business School Press.

Cahill, M. (1997, April 16–18). *Youth development and community development: Promises and challenges of convergence.* Paper presented at the Community and Youth Development: Complementary or Competing Priorities for Community Development Organizations, Princeton, New Jersey.

Camino, L. A. (2000). Youth-adult partnerships: Entering new territory in community work and research. *Applied Developmental Science, 4*(Supplement Issue).

Camino, L., & Zeldin, S. (2002). From periphery to center: Pathways for youth civic engagement in day-to-day life of communities. *Applied Developmental Science, 6*(3), 213–220.

Carbonaro, W. J., & Gamoran, A. (2002). The Production of Achievement Inequality in High School English. *American Educational Research Journal, 39*(4), 801–827.

Center for Research on the Context of Teaching. (2002). *Bay Area School Reform Collaborative; Phase One (1995–2001) Evaluation.* Stanford, CA: Stanford University.

Checkoway, B., Richards-Schuster, K., Abdullah, S., Aragon, M., Facio, E., Figueroa, L., Reddy, E., Welsh, M., & White, A. (2003). Young people as competent citizens. *Community Development Journal, 28,* 298–309.

Cochran-Smith, M., & Lytle, S. L. (1999). Relationships of knowledge and practice: Teacher learning in communities. *Review of Research in Education, 24.*

Colatos, A. M., & Morrell, E. (2003). Apprenticing urban youth as critical researchers: Implications for increasing equity and access in diverse urban schools. In B. Rubin & E. Silva (Eds.), *Critical voices in school reform: Students living through change.* London: Routledge Farmer.

Connell, J. P., Gambone, M. A., & Smith, T. J. (1998). *Youth development in community settings: Challenges to our field and our approach.* Rochester, NY: Institute for Research and Reform in Education.

Cook-Sather, A. (2001). Between student and teacher: Learning to teach as translation. *Teaching Education, 12*(2), 177–190.

Cook-Sather, A. (2002). Authorizing students' perspectives: Toward trust, dialogue, and change in education. *Educational Researcher, 31*(4), 3–14.

Copeland, M. (2003). The Bay Area School Reform Collaborative: Building the capacity to lead. In J. Murphy & A. Datnow (Eds.), *Leadership Lessons from Comprehensive School Reform Efforts.* Thousand Oaks, CA: Corwin.

Costello, J., Toles, M., Spielberger, J., & Wynn, J. (2000). History, ideology and structure shape the organizations that shape youth. In *Youth development: Issues, challenges, and directions* (pp. 185–231). Philadelphia: Public/Private Ventures.

Csikszentmihalyi, M., & Larson, R. (1984). *Being adolescent: Growth and conflict in the teenage years.* New York: Basic Books.

Cusick, P. A. (1973). *Inside high school: The student's world.* New York: Holt, Rinehart, and Winston.

Damico, S. B., & Roth, J. (1991). *The neglected dropout: General track students.* Paper presented at the American Educational Research Association, Chicago.

deCharms, R. (2001). Students need not be pawns. *Theory into Practice, 26*(4), 297–301.

Della Porta, D., & Diani, M. (1999). *Social movements: An introduction.* Malden, MA: Blackwell.

Denner, J., Meyer, B., & Bean, S. (2005). Young women's leadership alliance: Youth-adult partnerships in an all-female after-school program. *Journal of Community Psychology, 33*(1), 87–100.

Earl, L., & Lee, L. (1999). *Learning, for a change.* Paper presented at the American Educational Research Association, Montreal, April.

Eccles, J., & Gootman, J. A. (2002). *Community programs to promote youth development. Committee on Community-Level Programs for Youth.* Washington, DC: Board on Children, Youth, and Families, Commission on Behavioral and Social Sciences Education, National Research Council and Institute of Medicine. National Academies of Science.

Eccles, J. S., Midgley, C., Wigfield, A., Buchanan, C. M., Reuman, D., Flanagan, C., et al. (1993). Development during adolescence: The impact of stage-environment fit on young adolescents' experiences in schools and in families. *American Psychologist, 48*(2), 90–101.

Eckert, P. (1989). *Jocks and burnouts: Social categories and identity in the high school.* New York: Teachers College.

Elmore, R. (2000). *Building a new structure for school leadership.* Washington, DC: The Albert Shanker Institute.

Epstein, J. L., & Sanders, M. G. (1999). Connecting home, school, and community: New directions for social research. In M. Hallinan (Ed.), *Handbook of Sociology of Education.* New York: Plenum.

Ferguson, D. G. (1970, February 14–18). *The new morality of teenagers—The new student voice.* Paper presented at the American Association of School Administrators Convention, Atlantic City, NJ.

Fielding, M. (2001). Students as radical agents of change. *Journal of Educational Change, 2*(2), 123–141.

Fielding, M. (2004). Transformative approaches to student voice: Theoretical underpinnings, recalcitrant realities. *British Educational Research Journal, 30*(2), 295–311.

Fine, M. (1991). *Framing dropouts: Notes on the politics of an urban high school*. Albany: State University of New York Press.

Fine, M. (1993). [Ap]parent involvement: Reflections on parents, power and urban public schools. *Teachers College Record, 94*(4), 682–709.

Friend, M., & Cook, L. (2000). *Interactions: Collaboration skills for school professionals* (Third ed.). White Plains, NY: Longman.

Fullan, M. (1993). *Change forces*. New York: Falmer.

Fullan, M. G. (2001). *The new meaning of educational change*. (3rd ed.). New York: Teachers College.

Gamson, W. (1992). The social psychology of collective action. In A. Morris & C. Mueller (Eds.), *Frontiers in social movement theory* (pp. 53–76). New Haven: Yale University Press.

Ginwright, S. A. (2005). On urban ground: Understanding African-American intergenerational partnerships in urban communities. *Journal of Community Psychology, Vol. 33, No. 1, 101–110 (2005), 33*(1), 101–100.

Giroux, H. A. (1983). Theories of reproduction and resistance in the new sociology of education: A critical analysis. *Harvard Educational Review, 53*(3), 257–259.

Glaser, B., & Strauss, A. (1967). *The discovery of grounded theory*. Chicago: Aldine.

Goodenow, C. (1993). Classroom belonging among early adolescent students: relationship to motivation and achievement. *Journal of Early Adolescence, 13*(1), 21–43.

Goodwillie, S. (Ed.). (1993). *Voices from the future: Our children tell us but violence in America*. New York: Crown Publishers.

Grossman, P., Wineburg, S., & Woolworth, S. (2001). Toward a theory of teacher community. *Teacher College Record, 103* (6), 942–1012.

Heath, S. B., & McLaughlin, M. W. (Eds.). (1993). Identity and inner-city youth. New York: Teachers College.

Holdsworth, R., & Thomson, P. (2002). *Options within the regulation and containment of "student voice and/or Students researching and acting for change: Australian experiences.* Paper presented at the Annual Meeting of the American Educational Research Association, New Orleans.

Johnson, J. H. (1991). *Student voice motivating students through empowerment* (ED337875). Eugene: Oregon School Study Council.

Jones, K. (2004). *An assessment of community-based youth-adult relationships.* Unpublished dissertation. The Pennsylvania State University, Dept. of Agricultural & Extension Education.

Jones, K., & Perkins, D. (2004). Youth-adult partnerships. In C. B. Fisher & R. M. Lerner (Eds.), *Applied Developmental Science: An Encyclopedia of Research, Policies, and Programs.* Thousand Oaks, CA: Sage.

Kernaleguen, A. (1980). Clothing: An important symbol for adolescents. *School Guidance Worker, 35*(3), 37–41.

Kirshner, B., O'Donoghue, J. L., & McLaughlin, M. W. (Eds.). (2003). *New directions for youth development: Youth participation improving institutions and communities.* San Francisco, CA: Jossey-Bass.

Knight, T. (1982). *Youth advocacy report: A student initiated project (A report to the Vandalism Task Force).* Melbourne: Department of the Premier and Cabinet.

Kushman, J. W. (Ed.). (1997). *Look who's talking now: Student views of learning in restructuring schools.* (Vol. ED028257). Washington, DC: Office of Educational Research and Improvement.

Lareau, A. (1989). *Home advantage: Social class and parental intervention in elementary education.* Philadelphia: Falmer.

Larson, R., Walker, K., & Pearce, N. (2005). A comparison of youth-driven and adult-driven youth programs: Balancing inputs from youth and adults. *Journal of Community Psychology, 33*(1), 57–74.

Lashway, L. (2003). Distributed leadership. *Research Roundup, 19*(4).

Lee, L. E., & Zimmerman, M. (2001). *Passion, action, and a new vision for student voice: Learnings from the Manitoba School Improvement Program Inc.* Manitoba School Improvement Program, www.msip.ca.

Leonard, P. E., & Leonard, L. J. (2001). The collaborative prescription: remedy or reverie? *International Journal of Leadership Education, 4*(4), 383–399.

Levin, B. (2000). Putting students at the centre in education reform. *International Journal of Educational Change, 1*(2), 155–172.

Lieberman, A., & Wood, D. (2001). When teachers write: Of networks and learning. In A. Lieberman & L. Miller (Eds.), *Teachers caught in action: Professional development that matters* (pp. 174–187). New York: Teachers College.

Lieberman, A., & Grolnick, M. (1996). Networks and reform in American education. *Teachers College Record, 98*(1), 7–45.

Little, J. W. (1982). Norms of collegiality and experimentation. *American Educational Research Journal, 19*(3), 325–340.

Little, J. W. (1993). Teachers' professional development in a climate of educational reform. *Educational Evaluation and Policy Analysis, 15*(2), 129–151.

Louis, K. S., & Kruse, S. D. (1995). *Professionalism and community: Perspectives on reforming urban schools.* Thousand Oaks, CA: Corwin.

MacLeod, J. (1987). *Ain't no makin' it: Aspirations and attainment in a low-income neighborhood.* Boulder, CO: Westview.

Males, M. A. (1996). *Scapegoat generation: America's war on adolescence.* Monroe, Maine: Common Courage.

McLaughlin, M. W. (1993). Embedded identities: Enabling balance in urban contexts. In S. B. Heath & M. W. McLaughlin (Eds.), *Identity and inner-city youth* (pp. 36–68). New York: Teachers College.

McLaughlin, M. W., & Talbert, J. E. (1993). *Contexts that matter for teaching and learning: Strategic opportunities for meeting the nation's education goals.* Stanford University: Center for Research on the Context of Secondary School Teaching.

McLaughlin, M. W., & Talbert, J. E. (2001). *High school teaching in context.* Chicago: University of Chicago.

McLaughlin, M., Talbert, J., Kahne, J., & Powell, J. (1990). Constructing a personalized school environment. *Phi Delta Kappan, 72*(3), 230–235.

McLaughlin, M., & Mitra, D. (2004). *The cycle of inquiry as the engine of school reform: Lessons from the Bay Area School Reform Collaborative.* Stanford, CA: Center for Research on the Context of Teaching, Stanford University.

McLaughlin, M., Talbert, J., Park, G., White, C. R., Anderson, K., Beese, S., Copland, M., Ebby, R., Greeno, J., Ikeda, K., Imburg, J., Lin,

W., Mitra, D., Post, L., & Zarrow, J. (2000). *Assessing results: Bay Area School Reform Collaborative—Year 4.* Stanford, CA: Center for Research on the Context of Teaching, Stanford University.

Meyer, E. (1999). *Reshaping student-centered reform: A focus on students and teachers.* Unpublished dissertation. Stanford University, Stanford, CA.

Miles, M. B., & Huberman, A. M. (1994). *Qualitative data analysis.* Thousand Oaks, California: Sage.

Milofsky, C. (1988). Structure and process in community self-help organization. In C. Milofsky (Ed.), *Community organizations: Studies in resource mobilization and exchange* (pp. 183–216). New York: Oxford University Press.

Mitra, D. (2001). Opening the floodgates: Giving students a voice in school reform. *Forum, 43*(2), 91–94.

Mitra, D. L. (2003). Student voice in school reform: Reframing student-teacher relationships. *McGill Journal of Education, 38*(2), 289–304.

Mitra, D. L. (2004). The significance of students: Can increasing "student voice" in schools lead to gains in youth development? *Teachers College Record, 106*(4), 651–688.

Mitra, D. L. (2005). Adults advising youth: Leading while getting out of the way. *Educational Administration Quarterly, 41,* 3, pp. 520–553.

Mitra, D. L. (2006). Youth as a bridge between home and school: Comparing student voice and parent involvement as strategies for change. *Education and Urban Society.*

Mitra, D. L. (2007). Student voice in school reform: From listening to leadership. In D. Thiessen & A. Cook-Sather (Eds.), *International handbook of student experience in elementary and secondary school* (pp. 727–744). Dordrecht, The Netherlands: Springer.

Moore, M. (1997). *Crazy lives and crazy dreamers: Latina adolescents shaping selves in the inner city.* Unpublished dissertation, Stanford University, Stanford, CA.

Muncey, D., & McQuillan, P. (1991). *Empowering nonentities: Students in educational reform. Working paper #5.* Providence, RI: School Ethnography Project, Coalition of Essential Schools, Brown University.

National Research Council. (2002). *Community programs to promote youth development.* Washington, DC: National Academy.

Newmann, F. M., King, M. B., & Youngs, P. (2001). Professional development that addresses school capacity: Lessons from urban elementary schools. *American Journal of Education, 108* (4), 259–299.

Nightingale, E. O., & Wolverton, L. (1993). Adolescent rolelessness in modern society. *Teachers College Record, 94* (Spring), 472–86.

Noddings, N. (1992). *The challenge to care in schools: An alternative approach to education.* New York: Teachers College.

Oakes, J., & Lipton, M. (2002). Struggling for educational equity in diverse communities: School reform as a social movement. *Journal of Educational Change, 3*(3–4), 383–406.

O'Connor, C., & Camino, L. (2005). *Youth and adult leaders for program excellence: Youth participation in research and evaluation: Outcomes for youth.* Madison, WI: Community Youth Connection, University of Wisconsin Extension.

Oldfather, P. (1995). Songs "come back most to them": Students' experiences as researchers. *Theory into Practice, 34*(2), 131.

Pancer, S. M., Rose-Krasnor, L., & Loiselle, L. D. (2002). Youth conferences as a context for engagement. *New Directions for Youth Development, 96,* 47–64.

Panitz, T. (1996). *A definition of collaborative vs. cooperative learning.* Available online at: http://www.lgu.ac.uk/deliberations/collab.learning/panitz2.html.

Perkins, D. F., Borden, L. M., Keith, J. G., Hoppe-Rooney, T., & Villarruel, F. A. (2003). *Community youth development: Practice, policy, and research.* Thousand Oaks, CA: Sage.

Perkins, D., & Borden, L. (2003). Positive behaviors, problem behaviors, and resiliency in adolescence. In R. M. Lerner, M. A. Easterbrooks, & J. Mistry (Eds.), *Handbook of Psychology* (Vol. 6: Developmental Psychology). Hoboken, NJ: Wiley & Sons.

Pittman, K., & Cahill, M. (1992). *Pushing the boundaries of education: The implications of a youth development approach to education policies, structures, and collaborations* (Ed 366 880). Washington, DC: Academy for Educational Development.

Pittman, K., Irby, M., & Ferber, T. (2000). *Youth as effective citizens: Background report and recommendations.* Washington, DC: International Youth Foundation.

Pittman, K., & Wright, M. (1991). *Bridging the gap: A Rationale for enhancing the role of community organizations in promoting youth development*. Washington, DC: Carnegie Council on Adolescent Development.

Poplin, M., & Weeres, J. (1992). *Voices from inside the classroom*. Claremont, CA: The Institute for Education in Transformation at the Claremont Graduate School.

Powell, A. G., Farrar, E., & Cohen, D. K. (1985). *The shopping mall high school*. Boston: Houghton Mifflin.

Ragin, C. C., & Becker, H. S. (1992). *What is a case? Exploring the foundations of social inquiry*. New York: Cambridge University Press.

Roeser, R. W., Midgley, C., and Urdan, T. C. (1996). Perceptions of the school psychological environment and early adolescents' psychological and behavioral functioning in school: The mediating role of goals and belonging. *Journal of Educational Psychology, 88*(3), 408–422.

Roth, J., Brooks-Gunn, J., Murray, L., & Foster, W. (1998). Promoting healthy adolescents: Synthesis of youth development program evaluations. *Journal of Research on Adolescence 8*(4), 423–450.

Rudduck, J., & Flutter, J. (2000). Pupil participation and perspective: "Carving a new order of experience." *Cambridge Journal of Education, 30*(1), 75–89.

Rudduck, J. D., & Wallace, G. (1997). Students' perspectives on school improvement. In A. Hargreaves (Ed.), *Rethinking educational change with heart and mind (The 1997 ASCD Year Book)* (pp. 73–91). Alexandria, VA: Association for Supervision and Curriculum Development.

Ryan, R. M. & Powelson, C. L. (1991). Autonomy and relatedness as fundamental to motivation and education. *Journal of Experimental Education, 60*(1), 49–66.

Schmuck, P., & Schmuck, R. (1990). Democratic participation in small-town schools. *Educational Researcher, 19*(8), 14–19.

Scott, W. R. (1998). *Organizations: Rational, natural, and open systems* (4th ed.). Upper Saddle River, NJ: Prentice Hall.

Senge, P. M. (1994). *The fifth discipline: The art and practice of the learning organization*. New York: Doubleday.

Silva, E. (2003). Struggling for inclusion: A case study of students as reform partners. In B. Rubin & E. Silva (Eds.), *Critical voices in school reform: Students living through change* (pp. 11–30). London: Routledge Farmer.

Snow, D., & Benford, R. (1992). Master frames and cycles of protest. In A. Morris & C. McClurg Mueller (Eds.), *Frontiers in social movement theory* (pp. 133–155). New Haven: Yale University Press.

Soohoo, S. (1993). Students as partners in research and restructuring schools. *The Educational Forum, 57* (Summer), 386–393.

Stinson, S. W. (1993). Meaning and value: Reflections on what students say about school. *Journal of Curriculum and Supervision, 8*(3), 216–238.

Stokes, L. (2001). Lessons from an inquiring school: Forms of inquiry and conditions for teacher learning. In A. Lieberman & L. Miller (Eds.), *Teachers Caught in the Action: Professional Development That Matters. The Series on School Reform*. New York: Teachers College.

Strauss, A., & Corbin, J. (1994). Grounded theory methodology: An overview. In N. K. Denzin & Y. S. Loncoln (Eds.), *the handbook of qualitative research* (pp. 273–284). Thousand Oaks, CA: Sage.

Swap, S. M. (1993). *Developing Home-School Partnerships: From Concepts to Practice*. New York: Teachers College.

Takanishi, R. (Ed.). (1993). *Adolescence in the 1990s: Risk and opportunity*. New York: Teachers College.

Talbert, J. (1995). Boundaries of teachers' professional communities in U.S. high schools: Power and precariousness of the subject department. In L. S. Siskin & J.W. Little (Eds.), *The subjects in question: Departmental organization and the high school* (pp. 68–94). New York: Teachers College.

Thorkildsen, T. A. (1994). Toward a fair community of scholars: Moral education as the negotiation of classroom practices. *Journal of Moral Education, 23*(4), 371–385.

Villarruel, F. A., & Lerner, R. M. (Eds.). (1994). *Promoting community-based programs for socialization and learning*. San Francisco: Jossey-Bass.

Wehlage, G. G., Rutter, R. A., Smith, G. A., Lesko, N., & Fernandez, R. R. (1989). *Reducing the risk: Schools as communities of support*. London: Falmer.

Westheimer, J. (1998). *Among schoolteachers: Community, autonomy, and ideology in teachers' work*. New York: Teachers College.

Zeldin, S. (2004). Youth as agents of adult and community development: Mapping the processes and outcomes of youth engaged in organizational governance. *Applied Developmental Science, 8, 2*(75–90).

Zeldin, S., Camino, L., Calvert, M., & Ivey, D. (2002). *Youth-adult partnerships and positive youth development: Some lessons learned from research and practice in Wisconsin.* Madison: University of Wisconsin-Extension.

Zeldin, S., Camino, L., & Mook, C. (2005). The adoption of innovation in youth organizations: Creating the conditions for youth-adult partnerships. *Journal of Community Psychology, 33*(1), 121–135.

INDEX